Y0-DUS-050

Going Public

Going Public

A NOVEL

Muriel Dobbin

A Birch Lane Press Book
Published by Carol Publishing Group

To Ted
In memory of Phlange Welder

A Birch Lane Press Book
Published by Carol Publishing Group

Editorial Offices: 600 Madison Avenue, New York, N.Y. 10022
Sales & Distribution Offices: 120 Enterprise Avenue, Secaucus, N.J. 07094
In Canada: Musson Book Company, a division of General Publishing Co., Ltd., Don Mills, Ontario

Queries regarding rights and permissions should be addressed to Carol Publishing Group, 120 Enterprise Avenue, Secaucus, N.J. 07094

Carol Publishing Group books are available at special discounts for bulk purchases, for sales promotions, fund raising, or educational purposes. Special editions can be created to specifications. For details contact: Special Sales Department, Carol Publishing Group, 120 Enterprise Avenue, Secaucus, N.J. 07094

Manufactured in the United States of America

10 9 8 7 6 5 4 3 2 1

Library of Congress Cataloging-in-Publication Data

Dobbin, Muriel.
Going public : a novel / Muriel Dobbin.
p. cm.
"A Birch Lane Press book."
ISBN 1-55972-062-X :
I. Title.
PS3554.0145G65 1991
813'.54—dc20 90-32444
CIP

Going Public

Chapter One

Shopping for pink shoes didn't sound like a big deal, but it took up most of Tracy's morning and made her late for lunch with Pauline Ferry. She reflected, as she waved wildly for a taxi on Connecticut Avenue, that perhaps she'd been dawdling because she didn't want to meet Pauline, whom she'd greeted at parties for years, but who had never suggested lunch before. Tracy suspected that her friendship with First Lady Linda Potter, which rated an occasional mention in the gossip columns, was the reason for the invitation. She wondered why she never seemed able to say no.

Tracy hated it when she began questioning her social motivation in the middle of a traffic jam—that made it impossible for her to be anything except *very* late. It made her feel she ought to have had more faith in her horoscope, which that morning had advised her against leaping to conclusions and mentioned the importance of stopping to sniff the flowers along the way. Maybe she was leaping to a conclusion that she didn't like Pauline because she was feeling guilty about being late. Perhaps pink shoes qualified as taking time out for flowers.

It was the kind of soliloquy that got Tracy in trouble when she tried to share it with her husband, Tommy Gilmartin. He said she always began to chatter away when he was working on a tricky contract and needed all his wits about him. He said he never understood why someone who hardly drank at all could often sound as though she'd had three martinis.

If Tracy began to speculate on how the same discussion would have sounded if she *had* had three martinis, Tommy would get even more cross.

Tracy never understood why people weren't pleased when she paid attention to what they said. Her Mormon mother had told her that she could learn everything by listening, and her Southern father had told her nothing was more appealing than an attentive woman. Yet she sometimes thought people mostly wanted to hear themselves talk and didn't care whether you understood what they said or not. It seemed to her this was especially true in Washington, where she'd been listening a lot and not saying much for twenty years. Her husband talked a great deal—most public relations people did, she found—and her seventeen-year-old daughter, Rosemarie, held forth at length day and night on the superficiality of the world around her. Tracy probably would have said the same things at Rosemarie's age, except in her family nobody listened to anybody under thirty, let alone trusted them.

She'd tried to tell Rosemarie that, to let her know she wasn't the only person who'd felt frustrated and rebellious. Rosemarie said that was what she'd expect her mother to say, proving she hadn't listened to what Tracy had said. When Rosemarie went on to explain this was why she simply couldn't bond with her parents, Tracy thought of Krazy Glue and giggled, which made Rosemarie slam out of the room.

Sometimes Tracy wondered if she ought to be more assertive. When she asked Tommy about that, he grinned and said it might help if she ever said anything. Tracy said she liked to be agreeable, and he rubbed the back of her neck, as though scratching a puppy's ears.

She collected admirers like lint, and she remained a presence on the party circuit, not always at the most exclusive parties, until Sam Potter became President, when her social star soared, because the former Senate majority leader and his wife were old friends. Tracy had gone to work for Potter eight months after coming to Washington, giving rise to a rash of rumors that she was the latest acquisition of the senator, who made little secret of his womanizing. Again, it was a matter of suspicion that was never confirmed, because Tracy didn't talk and Potter bragged so much about his sexual prowess that nobody believed him. With the Potters she demonstrated her aptitude for becoming a friend of the family. When Tracy married handsome and prospering public relations man Tommy Gilmartin, the wedding was performed at the home of the Potters. When Tracy gave birth to a daughter nine months later, Linda Potter became her godmother.

Tracy and Tommy were a golden couple, but the stardust belonged to Tracy. She was a confection of a woman, her huge blue eyes dominating a heart-shaped face the way her bosom dominated her slender body. What made her different on the Washington scene was that nobody could recall hearing her say an unkind word about anybody. Many a battered veteran of the political and social wars had been lapped in Tracy's understanding, grateful for her throaty, appreciative laughter. She was as nice to women as she was to men, as Senator Eleanor McClusky of Illinois could testify.

And she was especially sympathetic to Tommy, which was why it worried her that he didn't seem to think she was as funny as he used to. Like this morning, when she had pink shoes and Pauline Ferry on her schedule, and she'd wandered downstairs in nothing but a big fluffy bath towel while Tommy was gulping coffee and rooting through his briefcase. Once he would have been amused, but now he apparently saw only a sleepy woman with nothing to do and nowhere to go.

"Aren't you dressed *yet*?" he asked. Tracy had smiled at him and stolen a sip of his coffee, which seemed to annoy him.

"What are you doing today?" he asked.

That was when she told him about the pink shoes and Pauline Ferry. That made more of an impression on him than her afternoon appointment with the principal at Rosemarie's school. He'd ducked her good-bye kiss, and she couldn't decide whether he was sulking or suffering from a stomachache. It upset Tracy when people weren't nice to her, and that was unusual for Tommy. Occasionally he was irritable, and she was understanding, because she suspected her disorganization could be exasperating. But he tended to tease rather than scold. Lately, he hadn't talked much, and that was hard, because she liked to listen to him more than to anyone else.

Tracy became aware that she wasn't listening to what was being said a few feet from her face.

"You *did* say Maison Blanche, didn't you?" the taxi driver repeated, and sighed as Tracy launched a search for her wallet in the depths of her purse. She apologized, overtipped, and smiled as she emerged from the taxi into a puddle. She was rewarded with a grin and a reminder that she'd left a package on the seat.

"Oh, my God, my pink shoes," she wailed. The driver's grin broadened.

Tracy could see Pauline Ferry's fresh-frozen smile over the shoulder of the headwaiter.

"I'm late," she murmured, and the headwaiter, who had known Tracy for years, nodded in a manner that suggested he had been made aware of her tardiness. Pauline was at her usual table, where she could see and be seen, but she disliked being kept waiting, especially by someone as insignificant as Tracy, even if she did have important friends.

Tracy was one of those people who straddled the bridge between the indestructible insiders like headwaiters and the press, who always survived Washington's political riptides, and the social pretenders, who waited in the shadows to see who emerged triumphant from the quadrennial presidential brouhaha. In previous years, Tracy had often fallen between the cracks, socially speaking. But currently she was on the White House list for invitations that went beyond formal functions and put her in the private theater for enchiladas and a movie with the President and the First Lady.

Pauline Ferry came from too much old money to worry about being in the social columns, but she did have Her Causes, as she called them, in a tone that made the capitalization clear. One of those causes was her husband, who had held positions of importance in two previous administrations and so far had achieved no notice in the current one because he'd never troubled to cultivate the Potters. Sam Potter's election had been a triumph of hardball politics, as a professional chewed up a glamorous amateur who had achieved fleeting glory in the primaries.

It was Pauline's money that had propelled Arthur Ferry's career, but even she couldn't do much about Sam Potter, not that she'd ever wanted to do anything about him before he reached the White House. The lunch with Tracy was one of the little sacrifices she made for Arthur and she resented the wait. She resented it even more as Tracy's arrival at her table was delayed by greetings from friends along the way. She was like a floor show, Pauline thought with distaste. Her smile encompassed the room, her blond bangs bounced and her walk was what somebody had defined as a sashay. Tracy's smile faded as she slid into the chair opposite Pauline, apologies tumbling from her lips.

"Tracy, dear," said Pauline. "Did you forget? Or were you just late again?"

Tracy wriggled like a child. "It was my pink shoes," she said.

"Pink shoes," Pauline repeated without surprise.

"Well, you know that dress I wore at Willie's party? The one with the merging peach and pink and gray, sort of?"

"The one that looked as if the colors had run?"

"Yes. Well, I was just determined to find shoes to wear with it. Gray didn't work. I always think that looks as though you have dirty feet. And peach is difficult to get the right dye, it always seems to come out salmon. So I thought pink would work but it had to be very pale. I mean, a lot of pinks are like those orchids that look hungry. So I was looking for this very pale pink and I was in five stores and then it was raining and I couldn't get a taxi . . . Pauline, I am so *very* sorry."

Tracy laid a small, warm hand on Pauline's silk-sheathed arm and bathed her in the full radiance of a smile that was hard to resist. Pauline shook her head and almost smiled.

"Tracy, you're impossible." But her voice was less glacial than usual. "Would you like a glass of wine?" she asked.

Tracy shook her head. "I'd love one, but I get so giddy, and I don't make sense, and I have to go talk to Rosemarie's school about why she dropped out and then go over to the Canadian embassy to meet Tommy at the reception for the new ambassador. Tommy has a couple of clients in Vancouver, you know."

Pauline didn't know and didn't care, but some response was necessary, she supposed. "Rosemarie dropped out of school?"

"She says she's being stifled by boring and irrelevant routine. She wants to be a revolutionary or something. She's at that age."

It occurred to Pauline that it might not be easy to have

Tracy for a mother. "So difficult," she murmured, and bent to the menu.

They were having coffee before the purpose of the lunch was revealed. Pauline had told Tracy all about the new club she was starting, to encourage "women of wealth and position," as she called them, to meet regularly to discuss social problems and what should be done about them. Tracy was fascinated, because she hadn't thought people still talked like that, and Pauline was pleased by her attentiveness.

"Perhaps you might like to join," Pauline said.

Tracy looked thoughtful, tracing the pattern in the white linen tablecloth with her finger. "That would be nice," she said, ignoring the voice inside her head which said it wouldn't, you don't want to lunch with her and you don't want to get together with those women who'll write checks for charity and spend the rest of the time rehashing who went where last week.

"Wonderful! We'll count on you," said Pauline, and moved on to her objective. "Do you suppose Linda Potter might be interested? I mean, she's always taken such an interest in the homeless—that kind of thing. . . ."

Here we go, Tracy thought. She should have taken longer with the pink shoes. "I don't know," she said. "I mean, I can't speak for Linda—"

"Of course not, of course not," Pauline interrupted. "But you and she are so close. Perhaps next time you're over at the White House informally, you might mention the idea. I mean, since you're going to be one of our little group, that would make her feel comfortable. . . ."

Tracy's smile gave no hint of her inward sigh. "I'll be happy to," she said. "But I don't know when I'll be seeing her again."

"I quite understand. And of course it's entirely up to her. But, you know, the First Lady has such influence, it could make such a difference to any projects we might take up.

And of course we'd be just delighted to have any suggestions from her."

It was Tracy's private opinion that it would be snowing in hell before Linda Potter, a woman of firm, not to say earthy, views, began playing patty-cake with the old Georgetown social set. And she really didn't know when she'd be invited back to the White House, in view of the gaffe she'd committed the last time, when she mixed up the date of the Potters' invitation. She'd tried to explain to them about her filing system, which was originally one of those lingerie holders with the days of the week embroidered on its compartments and which she kept hanging beside her bedroom mirror because she looked at that more often than at her desk. The invitation from the White House was in the wrong compartment. The President had laughed, especially when Tracy told him the filing system was a Christmas gift from Tommy that was probably meant to hold underpants. But Linda rolled her eyes.

Pauline was recounting a story about a dinner party where she had told Charley Dill, co-chairman of the Joint Committee on Intelligence, what to do about terrorism.

"Charley seemed quite impressed when I said what they ought to do was put a marine in uniform, with a gun, on every overseas flight. I mean, what do they all do when there isn't a war on, anyway? He said it was an intriguing idea. As a matter of fact, he said he'd like to get the reaction of the Marine Corps commandant."

Tracy was sure that *was* true.

"Such a fascinating man," Pauline continued. "I know he's a friend of yours, dear. And, of course, being up for reelection this year, he's quite cross with the President about all those base closings. And that's not all they're arguing abut, as I hear it. My husband—you know Arthur—said Charley and Sam had a terrible row about this Central American business and that awful man Filega. You know, Arthur is so plugged in to what's going on, I can't believe it.

I mean, the range of people who still call him for advice, you simply would not believe—"

Tracy, finishing her coffee, recognized that the second shoe had dropped. Arthur Ferry wanted another fancy job, and he hadn't paid his political dues with Sam Potter, so Pauline was doing some spadework. She wondered if Pauline seriously thought she could pull this off. On the other hand, Tracy had learned never to be surprised by what did work in Washington.

"I have to go," she said. Pauline seized the check, and Tracy let her. She felt she had earned lunch.

"So nice to have seen you," she told Pauline, her voice vivacious at the prospect of departure.

Pauline beamed at her as she signed the bill. "Dear Tracy," she said, "I can't imagine why we never did this before. Such fun. And I'll let you know when our first meeting is—so you can tell Linda in plenty of time."

By the time they reached the door of the restaurant, Tracy realized she'd forgotten the pink shoes again. She persuaded Pauline not to wait for her, and waved back at the hand flapping from the Ferry limousine. It was still raining, and Tracy abruptly decided she didn't feel like confronting a disapproving school principal who would probably cite lack of parental discipline as the root of Rosemarie's problems. She'd go home and have a hot bath and reschedule the appointment at the school. Then she'd see if the shoes matched the dress.

She leaned her head back on the seat of the taxi on the way home and wondered how she could get out of joining Pauline's club. Social Achievers, she'd said she was going to call it. S.A., Tracy thought, and giggled to herself. Socials Anonymous.

Tommy was home, to her surprise, and he seemed to be cleaning out his desk, which was even more of a surprise. He only did that about every five years on a rainy Sunday. He didn't seem glad to see her.

"I thought you were at Rosemarie's school," he greeted her.

"I just didn't feel like it. I'll call them."

"That won't impress them with your maternal dedication, will it?"

"I guess not." Tracy didn't feel like arguing. She began to climb the stairs and paused. "What're you doing home at this hour?"

"I—I needed some papers and I thought they might be in my desk. Why?"

"I just wondered. Well, that's fine. This way we can go to the embassy party together."

"I— Actually, I have to—to get back to the office. Have some errands. See you there."

He had turned back to his desk, and his voice was muffled. Tracy looked at him uncertainly for a moment, then went upstairs. She couldn't understand what was wrong with Tommy. He was usually so easygoing and genial. Maybe he'd lost a client. Maybe his business was in trouble, except only last week he'd been preening himself on three new clients. She sighed, and was grateful Rosemarie's door was open, signaling that its occupant was out. She didn't feel like dealing with Rosemarie any more than Rosemarie's school that day. Maybe it was the rain. She'd never liked rain.

She felt like going back to bed and starting over. Tommy's odd behavior nagged at her. They usually joked together. The best thing about their relationship, she'd always thought, was that they were friends. They talked to each other, although when she thought about it, it seemed like they hadn't been talking much lately. Maybe they needed a trip somewhere.

She unwrapped the pink shoes and was relieved to see they did match the dress. It was the first nice thing that had happened to her all day. Maybe she'd wear them that night. Except they'd get muddy in the rain and the dress was a little too dressed up. She started a tub, and while it ran, she wandered over to her closet and inspected its contents. She'd worn the dark blue silk last Tuesday and the red velvet on Wednesday. But this was Friday, so what had she worn Thursday?

She must have worn the blue silk twice that week. She wondered whether anyone had noticed. She pulled out her favorite black suede with the draped skirt and the heavy gold metal belt. Or there was the black silk with the beaded cuffs. She looked dramatic in black.

She almost fell asleep in the tub, and when she took a nap, she slept so long that when she roused, she realized she was going to be late for the reception. The house was dark and empty, and she chose the dramatic black to cheer herself up. She tried not to think about the fact she'd forgotten to call Rosemarie's school.

The warmth and brightness of the party revived her, and she was enjoying herself, chattering gaily, when a butler handed her a note. It was from Tommy. He'd been there early, it said, and had had to leave. He was having dinner with a client, and he'd be late. Tracy stared at the words in familiar handwriting and noticed that he'd left out his private signature of a broadly grinning face. The note didn't end *Love Tommy,* either.

Chapter Two

It was only a brief item in a gossip column in the Washington *Post*. It reported that Tracy Gilmartin, local socialite and friend of the famous and powerful, was negotiating with a New York publishing house for a book about her two decades as a woman about town in the nation's capital. It was greeted by the sound of faint snickering in both the salons and saloons of power, from the White House to Capitol Hill. Nobody could imagine Tracy writing a book. Everybody who was anybody liked Tracy; she was the pet of the party circuit. Even Jayne Millspaw, the Medusa of the establishment, could think of nothing more unkind to say about Tracy than that she seemed to have made a career out of being unable to say no. Eyebrows went up, heads were shaken, people laughed.

The hoarse chuckle of Charley Dill, U.S. senator from North Carolina and co-chairman of the Joint Committee on Intelligence, reverberated around his walnut-paneled private office as he thought about the idea. Pushing his glasses up on his forehead as his press secretary, Rob Klinger, read him the item, Senator Dill said he'd known Tracy a long time and he never expected her to be the author of anything more serious than a credit card receipt.

"Last time I saw her, she could barely remember her name," he recalled.

Klinger grinned. "That was that champagne reception at Kay's house."

"Right. And the damnedest thing was, I took her home because Helen was out of town and we talked half the night. And I mean *talked.* I must be getting old. Can't remember what we talked about, but that was all we did."

Dill shook his head regretfully and went back to fly-specking a speech on responsible foreign policy. Klinger reflected to himself that what the boss meant was *he* talked all night. After a few drinks, the only way to stop him from holding forth was to shoot him.

Four miles away, in a lavishly appointed house off Fox-hall Road, Linda Potter, wife of Samuel Perkins Potter, President of the United States, was asking her friend Jayne Millspaw what Tracy Gilmartin could possibly be writing about.

"Gossip," said Jayne succinctly.

Linda shook her beautifully frosted head. "Tracy can't remember her own telephone number. I know that for a fact. I mean, she's the most disorganized, the vaguest woman I ever met. She's the only person I know who either forgets she's been invited to the White House or loses the invitation."

Linda made clear that that had amused her. She laughed her tinkling laugh.

"We once actually sent a limousine to bring her to dinner and she was about to go somewhere else. She's funny and sweet and adorable, but write a book? She even gets the date wrong in her thank-you notes!"

Jayne tapped an inch-and-a-half-long coral fingernail against the pale porcelain of her teacup. "It does seem odd," she said thoughtfully.

"It's ridiculous," Linda retorted sharply. "That publishing house must be out of its mind. Who is it, anyway?"

"Wissip Golight. They got taken over a while back by that real estate tycoon who's trying to get himself recognized in literary circles. I read somewhere he was after what he called hot best-sellers."

"They're counting on Tracy for a hot best-seller?"

Jayne shrugged.

"Maybe they think they've latched on to somebody with insight into the Washington scene."

"Tracy's credentials for that aren't just unsubstantiated. They're nonexistent."

"Depends on how you look at her, I suppose. She knows a lot of people other people like to read about."

Linda's cup rattled in its saucer, and Jayne smiled.

"I'm sure Tracy would never— I mean, why would she?"

"It's usually called money."

Linda took a bite out of a cookie that wasn't on her diet. "Tracy is the soul of discretion. She's been around forever. My God, Sam and I were at her wedding. I'm Rosemarie's godmother. I cannot imagine—"

"Why are you so upset?" Jayne inquired silkily. "What does she have on you? Or Sam?"

"That's outrageous, Jayne."

"Linda," said Jayne wearily. "We've known each other since God was young. Don't play games with me. I know more about you than Tracy does. The difference is, I'm not writing a book about it."

The First Lady's face froze. "What do you mean, 'about it'?"

"I don't mean anything. I don't know what the book's about. But we've agreed it's not anything you'd expect Tracy to do."

"You've never liked her."

"I like her, all right. She's amusing and she always looks gorgeous and she can soothe ruffled feathers better than anybody I ever saw. But I'm always suspicious of anybody who's that goddamned sweet all the time. It isn't natural."

"Not for you, certainly."

"True. But you're not worried about me writing a book, either, are you, darling?"

Linda stood up, exasperated. "I have to go. Sam and I are going to that fund-raiser for AIDS victims tonight."

Jayne yawned, and poured herself another cup of tea. "So am I, so am I. See you there, I'm sure. Are you going to ask Sam what he thinks about Tracy's book?"

"I really don't care and I'm sure he'll pay no attention. It's probably a party recipe book."

During the limousine ride back to the White House, Linda concentrated on what she should wear to the fund-raiser. Something not too bright and gay—she winced briefly at the thought. Yet not black, which might seem ghoulish. Maybe the dark blue with the inset glimmer in its folds. Like a gleam of hope. That might strike the right note.

She sighed. Perhaps she and Sam could have a drink before they went to the dinner. Or she could have a drink. He worried about drinking now, except just before they went to bed, which didn't exactly make him a playful partner. There had been times when he'd indulged in a martini or two before making a speech and he'd got people and places confused. He also sometimes sounded as though his tongue had been knitted.

As it turned out, the President was kept late at a meeting with the secretary of state, and by the time he appeared in the family sitting room, Linda was dressed and drinking a glass of wine while she read a copy of *The Washingtonian* in which she had just found another announcement that Tracy Gilmartin was writing a book. She smiled absently as her husband kissed her on the cheek and said her dress was just right. He always said that, she reflected. "Right." Not lovely, or becoming, or sexy. But politically "right." That was something men didn't have to worry about on formal occasions. It was either black or white tie, which narrowed your options.

"Did you see this about Tracy Gilmartin?" She held out the magazine.

He scanned it a little impatiently, then frowned. "What in God's name would little Tracy write that anybody'd want to publish?"

He glanced at his watch and signaled to the butler for a glass of wine. His forehead was faintly creased.

"Jayne Millspaw and I were wondering the same thing this afternoon. She saw it in the *Post*."

The President took a healthy swallow of his wine. He always drank wine as though it were beer, she thought. It was a characteristic that grated on her. "Maybe it's a joke book," he suggested.

"The wit and wisdom of Tracy Gilmartin?"

Their matching smiles were small.

"Jesus, you don't suppose she's writing one of those kiss-and-tell things, do you?"

"That would be interesting," Linda said.

"Set this town on its ear." He finished his wine.

"Why?"

"Come on. Because Tracy's screwed just about everybody in three administrations, that's why."

"Including you, darling?"

"Don't be silly."

He had another glass of wine before they left.

"Why would Tracy want to do such a thing?" Linda asked in the limousine. She noticed she didn't have to explain what she was talking about.

"She probably isn't doing any such thing," he said.

"What's interesting is that we're talking about it. That's exactly what her publisher has in mind. Like those tabloids with the teaser headlines and stories that don't live up to the promise."

She felt his eyes on her in the dimness.

"What are *you* worried about, anyway? She's straight, isn't she?"

"Sam—" Her voice was sharp.

"I'm teasing you, honey." He patted her on the knee, and she jerked her leg away, then looked fixedly out of the window as the car came to a smooth halt outside the hotel where the dinner was being held. She arranged her face in her political smile, and they moved into the ballroom with the customary covey of Secret Service and VIP greeters.

Fortunately, it was the kind of evening when she was supposed to look solemn. The subject was grim, and so were the speeches. There was an eight-year-old guest with AIDS, who brought tears to everybody's eyes. The little boy, pale and angelic in a gray flannel suit, was obviously shy as he trotted up to the head table, clutching his father's hand. Watching him, Linda saw the child's face suddenly brighten into a smile directed toward a table on his left. She focused on a shining blond head and a smile so warm that it had comforted the child. Linda recognized Tracy Gilmartin, swathed in pale yellow chiffon. The combination of colors made her look as though she were floating in a golden aura.

As though aware of Linda's gaze, Tracy looked up, and her hand came up in a tiny wave. Linda smiled but didn't wave back, and immediately felt ashamed of herself. She couldn't believe Tracy would do anything unkind. Nobody had ever heard Tracy say an uncharitable word about anyone, which was a lot more than she could say about Jayne Millspaw, whose laser tongue scarified even her friends. Linda found herself watching Tracy, who was listening and reacting enthusiastically to those around her.

Linda noticed that Tracy, unlike her tablemates, didn't talk through the speeches, or even the introduction of the speakers. She seemed genuinely interested. Thinking back, Linda realized what she liked most about Tracy was the way she gave you her full attention. She listened, and when she responded, she seemed to have given thought to what you said. When Linda thought about it, that was hardly a characteristic of a dingbat, which was how a lot of people dismissed Tracy. Never had a word of anything she'd told Tracy percolated back to her on the capital grapevine, one of the most active in the world.

Looking at Tracy and remembering how long they had been friends, Linda chided herself. The way to solve the nagging doubt created by the announcements of Tracy's book was simply to ask her what it was about. It was the obvious open thing to do, and that was why Jayne probably never would have thought of it. Jayne lived on the dark side of the moon. Linda felt better and smiled cheerfully at Sam, who looked a little taken aback but returned the smile. There was to be a small private reception after the dinner, and with a word to the chairman Linda made sure Tracy would be invited to join it. He knew Tracy, of course, and he smiled and nodded.

With her eyes trained to register who came and went at social gatherings, Linda saw Tracy arrive, bestowing one of her radiant smiles on the Secret Service agent at the door, who almost forgot himself and smiled back.

Linda noticed that Tommy Gilmartin wasn't with Tracy and wondered briefly where he was. Tommy rarely missed a social outing, and usually hovered around Tracy for a while before drifting away. Tracy not infrequently was escorted home by someone else, and there was always someone available, but she defended Tommy's disappearances, attributing them to his conscientious cultivation of potential clients as well as his inclination to have a nightcap with one of the boys and forget the time.

Linda had thought occasionally that it was a rather odd marriage, but hadn't given it any more thought than that, because so few marriages weren't odd. At least Tracy never complained or criticized Tommy. When they were together, they seemed to be amiable and enjoying each other's company. Linda realized she didn't know that much about Tracy's personal life, not nearly as much as Tracy knew about hers.

The flicker of doubt rose again, and Linda waved at Tracy, who came toward her, moving with that graceful walk where you had to look for the wiggle, which most men did. They brushed cheeks carefully in the social nonkiss that preserved makeup and was noncommittal in terms of affection.

"Wasn't that little boy precious? It's so sad," Tracy said.

"You were the only one who got a smile out of him," Linda told her.

Tracy beamed. "I wanted to hug him."

"Maybe he's not accustomed to that reaction anymore, unfortunately."

Tracy shook her head, then looked at Linda a touch reproachfully. "How have you been? I haven't seen you in a month. Are you still mad at me because I forgot that dinner?"

Linda didn't want to hear again about Tracy's filing system. "We're keeping you for something special," she assured her.

"Something or somebody?" Tracy's eyes sparkled.

Linda suddenly remembered the last time they had spent a lengthy and somewhat liquid evening discussing their love life. Or her love life. She felt a little uncomfortable at the recollection.

"My dear, what's this I'm reading about you? You're writing a book? About what?"

Tracy threw back her head and laughed. "Oh, my God, it's so ridiculous! This nice editor I know thinks I should write sort of a social history. You know, parties I remember, that kind of thing? I think he's crazy. I'm not that interesting. I can't imagine who'd read it."

"Well, I expect it would depend on what parties you remembered," Linda said cautiously.

Tracy laughed again and patted Linda's arm. "I don't know anything's going to come of it. I guess I was flattered he thought I was interesting enough to write a book."

"I thought maybe you were doing one of those how-to-entertain books," said Linda.

"I don't entertain that much, darling. People are nice enough to entertain me, most of the time."

"That's because you're such a great guest. When you remember to show up!"

They both laughed, and Linda saw nothing but candor in Tracy's clear blue eyes.

"So you aren't sure whether you will write a book or not?" she asked.

"I'm not certain, really. But Jerry—that's the editor—is quite enthusiastic. He says a lighter view of social history would sell because it would be different. I guess he knows what's doing, and it might be fun. Give me something to do."

"But you're always so busy, rushing here and there. It's hard to reach you. When will you find time?"

Tracy hesitated before she answered. "I can find time," she said. "And I could use some extra money."

Linda studied the vivacious face and noticed faint shadows beneath Tracy's eyes. "Where's Tommy tonight?" she asked.

Her question was casual, but it seemed to her there was a brief darkening of the smooth tranquillity of Tracy's lovely face.

"Oh"—her voice was light, but it had lost its lilt—"he's out of town." She touched Linda's arm gently. "I ought to go say hello to Sa—the President. See you soon?"

Linda nodded and wondered if she had imagined an uncharacteristic abruptness in the way Tracy turned and walked away. She disappeared into the flow of women in silks of many colors and men who looked like moderate- to well-tailored penguins.

Chapter Three

The telephone still rang a lot, and heavily embossed, ivory-tinted invitations still fell through the mailbox, but Tracy Gilmartin's world had turned upside down and there didn't seem to be a soul she could tell about it. Her party face remained more or less intact, but she cried when she went back to the empty house on Roxbury Street, especially when she tried to take stock of her financial situation. She could hardly remember the days when pink shoes preoccupied her, yet it wasn't long ago that all her worries seemed to involve keeping her social calendar straight. All that ended the day Tommy, her husband of eighteen years, announced he was leaving her to go and live in a house by a lake in British Columbia with the love of his life, whose name turned out to be Raymond.

Tracy still thought she'd behaved in a civilized manner when Tommy broke the news to her.

"Raymond?" she said.

"Raymond," her husband replied.

"I've always liked the name," Tracy observed, mostly because she was trying to think of something to say that didn't involve bursting into tears. Tommy made a sound of exasperation.

"I suppose you want to invite him to a dinner party as part of the family?" he asked.

Tracy blinked and considered. It was easier, she found, to act as though he'd said nothing out of the ordinary. "I suppose he is going to be part of the family—at least, of your family?"

"If I told you I was going to have myself shot from a cannon," said Tommy, "you'd ask what I was going to wear."

"I don't understand why you're being so unpleasant," Tracy insisted. "Would you prefer it if I had hysterics and threw a tantrum?"

"I suppose in a way I would," said her husband. "In all the years we've been married, I've never heard you raise your voice or seem to get mad. It's as if nothing matters enough to you for you to get upset about it. And that includes me."

"I always thought we got along very well."

"I never knew you thought about it at all. I remember after your father died, your mother told me they'd never had an argument and she sort of wished they had."

Tracy wondered how long Tommy had been nurturing this currently blooming hostility toward her.

"My parents were very fond of each other, as far as I know," she said quietly. "They also put a premium on civilized behavior. Practically the worst thing I could do as a child was to be rude or raise my voice. My father was a most considerate man. He even took my mother and me out separately to dinner and the theater so he could pay the proper amount of attention to each of us. He was the most thoughtful man I ever met. Certainly the most polite."

"And you're exactly like him. There's nothing you won't do to avoid trouble. No wonder they call you Tracy the soft touch."

Tracy's eyes widened in puzzlement.

"Who calls me that?"

"It doesn't matter. It's true, isn't it? In more ways than one." The telephone rang and Tracy picked it up gratefully.

"Yes. Yes, this is she. I do? No, no, nothing wrong. I have a little headache. I'm sorry, didn't I RSVP? I'd love to come. Yes. No, I'm afraid he—he's going to be out of town for a while. Yes, he'll be sorry to miss you too. See you Tuesday then."

"Who was that?" Tommy asked.

"Dorrie Milliken. Dinner party."

"Pete Milliken the lawyer's wife? Fine, you can kill two birds and talk to him about a divorce."

Tracy rubbed hard at a smudge on the polished wood of the telephone table. "Why should we get a divorce?" she asked. "I mean, what's going to be so different? We've had what I thought was a pleasant arrangement for years, and I don't know why you didn't tell me about Raymond instead of skulking about with him."

She hesitated, then looked Tommy in the eye. "It's not as if you've ever had . . . all that much interest in sleeping with *me.*"

"I knew you'd bring that up."

"Wouldn't it have been very odd if I hadn't brought it up, under the circumstances?"

Tracy thought she'd made the best of a situation others might have given up on. The most surprising aspect of Tommy's announcement was that he was interested in sex with anybody. Their courtship had been distinguished by remarkable restraint on his part, and their honeymoon by a degree of abstention from intimate physical contact that often left Tracy alone in their hotel bedroom while Tommy had a nightcap that lasted until the bar closed downstairs and she was asleep. When she woke up, what he wanted to play was tennis.

Tommy's behavior was mystifying to Tracy, who was

then twenty-one and had never lacked for attention from the opposite sex. She was pretty, she was amusing, and she knew how to listen. She had been brought up to pay attention to what people said. Her father was a Southerner who was liberal in politics but nostalgic for iron-magnolia women. Her mother was a Mormon with a guilty conscience about abandoning the Latter-Day Saints. Her upbringing of her daughter owed a good deal to her recollections of pioneer women who stood by their men, and although Tracy never absorbed her mother's domestic skills, she emerged from her childhood a conflicting mixture of courtesy and coquettishness that made her something of an anachronism.

Tracy sometimes thought she'd married Tommy because he was the only man she'd dated who hadn't constantly asked her to go to bed with him. She hadn't discussed that aspect of his personality with her father, but she had mentioned to her mother how much Tommy seemed to respect her. That promptly established him forever in her mother's good graces, and looking back on it, she reflected that she'd probably talked to the wrong parent.

It wasn't as though she'd gone to bed with all the people who'd asked her, but she'd always felt bad about refusing. Saying no nicely came from her father's teachings. Saying no at all was inherited from her mother. And to find that Tommy, tall, handsome, merry-faced Tommy, was willing to cuddle her, but would just as soon not make love to her, except on rare occasions when he seemed to be steeling himself to it, perplexed Tracy more than it upset her. She assumed there was something wrong with *him,* and felt sorry for him. When her initial advances were met with a kiss on the cheek and a turn of the back, she didn't ask why. She decided the best thing to do was become good friends with him in hopes he might feel comfortable enough with her to tell her what the problem was. She supposed it should have occurred to her he was homosexual, but she found the idea illogical. Why would he marry someone like her if he preferred to sleep with a man?

Tommy was more domestic than she was, planning the decor of their house and cooking gourmet dinners, but he wasn't much of a family man. He showed restrained affection for their daughter, Rosemarie, the product of a midnight when Tommy was drunk enough to overcome his customary aversion to sex. He'd never talked to Tracy about why their sexual life was almost nonexistent. On the few occasions she tried to bring it up in conversation, he had become silent or gone out for a drink.

Yet apart from that, Tommy was kind, funny, and charming, and they enjoyed each other's company, or Tracy had thought they did. They'd always laughed a lot together, and he'd always been delighted with her skill at finding him business contacts in the course of her social rounds.

He'd worked hard to build up his public relations business. He'd done so well, he'd been asked to merge with one of the largest firms in the country, joining them as an executive vice president. He'd taken Tracy out to celebrate that, and she remembered it because it was such an odd evening. After dinner, he'd explained he had to meet with one of his new firm's New York operatives who was making a stopover at Dulles Airport en route to Los Angeles. It would be a bore for her to go out there, and he wouldn't be long. He'd driven her home and hadn't returned until dawn, grumbling about delayed flights.

"That night you joined Jones and Crowther," Tracy said suddenly, "when you went to Dulles. Or you said you went to Dulles. That was Raymond."

Tommy nodded, and looked at her a little sheepishly. "You remembered that?"

"I remember more than you think," she said sadly.

"Tracy"—his voice was softer—"I'm sorry. I didn't want to hurt you. I should have told you. It's just that— Well, I didn't think you— Well, you were always so busy. And—you did have an active social life of your own, to be candid, didn't you?"

Tracy picked up an emery board and smoothed a ragged edge on a fingernail. Fingernails could be a lifesaver when you didn't want to look at someone, and it was true that she had decided Tommy's continuing uninterest in her body freed her to some extent from the bonds of monogamy. She always had offers.

"We never talked about—our problem," she said at last.

"I know. And we should have. Would it have made any difference?"

"I don't know now." She suddenly felt drained of emotion. She didn't even know why she was surprised. She felt like a fool. "I guess that's all," she said. "When do you want to move out?"

"Oh, any time. I mean, maybe next week. And I won't be taking anything but my clothes. A few books and records maybe."

"Won't you need stuff for your new house? I mean, you're welcome to take—"

"No, no. Raymond—Raymond has very definite taste in interiors."

Tracy suddenly saw a vignette from the past in her mind's eye. "Raymond," she remembered. "The Raymond at Blues Corner? The pianist?"

"Yes."

Tracy smiled bitterly, recalling how often they had gone there for drinks after dinner. Tommy had always wanted to sit at the piano bar. The pianist was a slender, brown-eyed young man who never seemed to wear anything except black suede jumpsuits. Tracy had commented merrily once or twice on his passion for black suede. Perhaps that was how he would decorate the house for Tommy. Black suede walls? She looked around the comfortable room with its worn leather sofa and laden bookshelves and Tommy's beloved bentwood rocker and fought back tears. She stood up and moved toward the door. Tommy hovered beside her.

"Tracy, I don't want you to suffer. I mean, we might have to sell the house, but I'll help out as much as I can. I'll be a little strapped because I'm—really starting out fresh. A new life."

"You don't have clients in British Columbia?"

He shook his head.

"You're giving up your work here?"

"Well, sort of. Like a sabbatical."

"Oh, for God's sake," said Tracy. She went upstairs and closed the door of their bedroom in Tommy's anxious face. She looked in the mirror and was pleased to see she looked the same, although God knew what was fermenting beneath that smooth surface. She glanced at the calendar and noticed she was supposed to go to a cocktail party that evening. She'd concentrate on that. She'd think about Tommy later.

She was critically appraising a new black silk suit with a skirt that showed more of her legs than usual when Rosemarie walked in. She had never managed to persuade Rosemarie that knocking on a door was merely discreet, not evidence of bourgeois decadence.

"Hello, darling," she said cheerfully.

Rosemarie had her mother's looks but you couldn't always find them. Her thick blond hair sprang from her head in a manner suggesting she'd just been electrocuted, her blue eyes were sullen, her face didn't look clean, and she was wearing her usual uniform of skimpy T-shirt and ragged jeans. On her feet were grubby sneakers. She regarded her mother with the unctuous disapproval reserved for the young and the righteous.

"You're going *out*?"

Tracy wondered why both her husband and her daughter appeared astounded and almost offended that she was contemplating neither suicide nor a nunnery.

"Uh-huh. Little party at the Boglers'. Where you off to?"

"A political meeting." Rosemarie's voice left no doubt about the importance of her evening.

"That's nice," said Tracy, aware the remark would annoy her daughter.

"The Committee for the Condemnation of American Policy in Central America. Jared thinks I ought to learn more before I go down there."

"Down where?" Tracy asked as she applied hyacinth blue eye shadow.

"I told you. I'm committed to the revolution. Jared wants me to join him. I *told* you, but you were so hysterical about my dropping out of that ridiculous school."

Tracy's mind focused and dissolved into a flashback. Rosemarie had so many crises, so many causes, delivered so many pronunciations, that it was hard to keep track of them. But the name "Jared" touched a chord.

"Jared Filega?"

"Of course."

"Of course," Tracy repeated softly, and, inaudibly, "he was always committed to reworking the world as he saw it."

She remembered Jared Filega from the days when he was a student at Georgetown Law School. A tall, brooding, intense young man, he had slipped briefly into frivolity under the influence of champagne served by his law professor at a Christmas party to which Tracy had been invited. She smiled faintly as she recalled walking through the snowy streets with Jared, dodging his snowballs, frolicking in the snow, and falling into bed with him at his studio apartment. It had been one of those accidental interludes she still remembered. The memory made her smile, although it had turned out that Jared offered little reason to smile. He displayed a distressing propensity for violence that was not limited to his passion for social change. That was Rosemarie's Jared.

"You *have* heard of him?" Rosemarie was asking.

Tracy nodded. "I have."

Rosemarie paused, apparently changed her mind about delivering another lecture, and fiddled with the perfume bottles on her mother's dressing table.

"He told me," said Tracy, taking pity on her daughter's embarrassment.

A flicker of anxiety crossed Rosemarie's pale face. "How are—did you—?"

"I was surprised. Mostly that he didn't tell me before. I suppose I didn't want to admit there were problems. I guess he didn't either."

"You're not upset?"

"Maybe a little. I don't like being deceived for a long time. But there isn't much I can do about it, is there? I mean, I can hardly compete with—Raymond, can I?" Tracy's voice sharpened briefly.

"He—he is a little odd," Rosemarie admitted.

"How long have you known?" It stung Tracy that her daughter had been told first.

"I—met him a while back."

Tracy turned back to the mirror and carefully applied lipstick to conceal her feelings. "I want him to be happy," she said after a moment. "Just as I want you to be happy, darling."

"You really *don't* care, do you, Mother?"

Tracy rejected one pair of carved gold earrings for another, ignoring Rosemarie's expression of scorn. "I don't like to make a fuss. You know that."

"I give up." The door slammed behind Rosemarie, as usual, and Tracy sighed, even as she took pleasure in her own appearance in the mirror.

On the stairs, she passed Tommy, whose face registered surprise.

"You're going *out*?"

She smiled as brightly as she could. "Of course. Give Raymond a kiss for me. Darling."

She took satisfaction in his open-mouthed reaction as she closed the front door quietly behind her.

She knew practically everybody at the Boglers' party, including Willie Temple, maverick scion of a publishing empire, who has spent most of his life being intimidated by his father and fleeing a series of irate wives. Tracy and Willie had been friends since she rescued him from an embassy garden party during which his first wife upended a bowl of punch over his head. Tracy, who was leaving, saw the bedraggled form scurrying down the drive and opened her car door. Since that time, the two had been occasional lovers, although that tended to happen more by accident than by design, because Willie said he had no luck with women he slept with, and couldn't afford to lose a friend. He was delighted to see Tracy at the Boglers' because he was going through his third divorce and wanted to tell her what That Woman had done to him. He persuaded her to come to dinner with him in his apartment that occupied the entire top floor of a building overlooking Rock Creek Park and Tracy didn't mind. She was beginning to think she'd like to tell someone what That Man had done to her, which was something she'd never done before. A few hours later, they were sharing an outsize velvet sofa in Willie's drawing room and his head was on her shoulder.

"Willie," she said, "can I talk to you?"

"Mmmmm," said Willie, who had talked himself out, and was more interested in nosing his way into her décolletage. Tracy shifted a little, and he looked up at her with surprise.

"Sorry, darling. I do something wrong?"

"No, no." Tracy patted his well-tanned cheek. "I'm unhappy, Willie."

He sat up. "Who did it? Tell me and I'll bankrupt him."

"My husband."

"Oh." Willie sighed. The ground was too familiar and painful for him to concede it to anyone else, even Tracy.

"Dear, dear Tracy," said Willie. "How could anyone be

unkind to anyone as kind and beautiful as you? You need someone to take care of you." He wrapped his arms around her, and Tracy sighed and offered no objection. She wasn't sure she wanted to talk about Tommy, but it would have been nice if Willie had been willing to listen. While he undressed her, it crossed her mind it was nice somebody wanted her. She put her arms around Willie's neck and thrust away the image of her mother's outraged Mormon face. When she went home, shortly before dawn, she found Tommy had moved into the guest room and Rosemarie had moved out, leaving a brusque note adjuring her parents to join the real world. A week later, Tommy was gone as well, leaving a curt note with his new address in British Columbia. Tracy sat staring at the two letters. They reminded her of epitaphs. For the first time that she could remember, she was alone.

That was why she was so pathetically grateful when Clayton Clapper called to invite her to lunch, and she discovered that someone not only thought she was interesting, but also considered her life fascinating enough to be a book that people would read. She didn't quite believe it, but it was enormously comforting to think about, especially when she discovered it might make her some money. Her father would have approved, she thought. He considered Scarlett O'Hara an eminently practical woman.

Chapter Four

Clayton Clapper had been an investigative reporter in Washington for seventeen years. He had a reputation as a conscientious and painstaking digger through files and documents. His years of grubbing in the financial and moral garbage of the powerful had not culminated in his finding the golden pot of scandal that would catapult him to fame on the talk shows, as well as provide him with financial security. Approaching his fortieth year, aware every time he looked in the mirror that frustration was carving deep lines in his chubby face, Clayton knew it was now or most likely never. His writing showed his desperation. The leads of his stories and columns increasingly promised more than their content delivered, as his editors pointed out. Clayton could offer no argument.

"You're jumping the gun more than you used to," an editor told him after reading Clayton's latest denunciation of skullduggery in the Pentagon.

"You've got to nail down this kind of thing more. Nowadays we can't go on your gut feelings, although you're probably right."

"The First Amendment," the editor added regretfully, "isn't what it used to be. We're all worried about lawsuits."

Clayton acknowledged his weaknesses. He'd played catch-up in scandal stories, unearthed some good angles, but he'd never unveiled a Watergate or an Irangate. He'd never come close to toppling an official more elevated than a right-wing under secretary of state who was such a target of overkill by the press that the story didn't even rate a mention in the evening newscast.

He was discouraged in mind and lethargic in body the day he met Tracy Gilmartin at the Occidental Grill for lunch. Like his peers, he enjoyed Tracy's company, and he did not share the conventional journalistic wisdom that she was a dishy dingbat with great contacts. A dingbat babbled, in Clayton's experience. He'd been married to one of those and hadn't contemplated matrimony since. His former wife had taught him the value of silence. In fourteen years, she'd never made sense. Even worse, she'd constantly repeated her clichés. Barbie had talked all the time she was awake, and when she took to talking in her sleep, Clayton's patience gave out. Their divorce was amiable. Their marriage had never been distinguished by physical intensity or even by any degree of communication. They had drifted into matrimony as a result of a pleasant long weekend together at a hotel on Maryland's Eastern Shore, during which they didn't realize they had exhausted everything either wanted to know about the other. Flushed by the success of the weekend, they rushed to the altar, and the marriage was over almost before it began.

Tracy appealed to Clayton for the same reason she appealed to the rest of the press. She was exceedingly attractive, and she adored reporters. She thought they were funny and told wonderful stories that they couldn't publish about people whom she knew better than the reporters did. She never confirmed those stories, but she laughed a lot.

"She doesn't have the brains to realize what she knows," said an exasperated columnist who invested a dinner in Tracy and emerged with nothing but the bill. Clayton didn't agree.

Tracy would comment and interject appropriately, he noticed, but it was as if she were programmed simply to listen. He wondered if she might be reprogramed, but he'd never been able to figure out how. He refused to attribute her popularity to her having screwed everybody in the capital. He suspected she didn't sleep around as much as she was said to. If she had, he observed, she wouldn't have had time for lunches or dinners. He also was interested in her enduring friendships with political movers and shakers who apparently trusted her. Tracy *had* to have stored in her head tidbits about political, diplomatic, and corporate deals. Clayton considered her a long-term investment.

She was late for lunch, as usual. When she arrived, chic in a red raincoat of some lustrous material, wearing outrageously high-heeled shoes, he noticed the aquamarine eyes peering out from under her trademark bangs looked tired. Her greeting was warm, yet she gave an impression of being unusually subdued. She rippled, but she didn't bubble, and she accepted a glass of wine before lunch, instead of her usual mineral water.

"How's Tommy?" Clayton asked by way of small talk. To him astonishment, her eyes filled with tears.

"Tracy, what's wrong? Has something happened to Tommy?"

She took a sip of wine and shook her head. Clayton glanced around, grateful for the shelter of their booth, then leaned over and patted her hand.

"Tell me about it, sweetie. You can tell me. We're old friends," he told her gently. Tracy began to cry in earnest. Clayton handed her his handkerchief and studied the menu. After a moment or two, he raised his eyes and found her looking at him with tearful gratitude. She reached over and took his hand.

"Clayton, I can't tell you how much that meant to me," she said brokenly. "Nobody ever seemed interested in hearing my problems before. It was sweet of you to say something like that just to make me feel better."

"Hell, I meant it," he said. "You've listened to me often enough. If you've got troubles, you can talk to me. I'll even cross my heart and hope to die I won't tell anybody else."

He grinned at her and was rewarded by a small, hiccuping giggle. Tracy took another sip of wine, choked, and picked up her glass of ice water. Clayton waited, shaking his head at a hovering waiter, who nodded and drifted away. He wondered what had caused Tracy such distress. He'd never seen her cry before, except in sympathy for somebody else's sad story. Tracy was fun; that was her stock-in-trade. Tracy in tears was unheard of. Something about Tommy; maybe he was sick. Cancer, or something like that. Clayton liked Tommy, whom he considered a quintessential public relations man, full of good cheer and good talk without being too brash. He and Tracy seemed to have one of those convenient marital arrangements that permitted them to go their separate social ways, yet remain a couple. Clayton pressed the small, slender hand that lay in his. There was a childlike quality to Tracy that he'd never seen before. She usually reminded him of Goldie Hawn, but today she looked more like Marilyn Monroe.

"Talk to me," he urged. Tracy looked at him with eyes like blue puddles.

"Tommy's gone," she said, and abruptly picked up the menu.

"Crab crepes," she said with a sniff.

Clayton took the menu away from her. "Never mind that for a minute. What do you mean, he's gone? Gone where?"

"British Columbia."

"On a trip?"

"With Raymond."

"Raymond?"

"Raymond. That's his lover." A tear splashed on the tablecloth.

Clayton frowned at the waiter, who was unabashedly eavesdropping. "Tommy's gone to British Columbia with his lover. For good?"

She nodded. "And Rosemarie's gone to Central America to join Jared Filega."

"Filega!"

"Yes."

"You have to be joking. No? Couldn't you stop her?"

"If I'd told her I had an affair with Jared when he was a student at Georgetown, that would only make her despise me more, not love him less. Jared has a deal going with that mad colonel Sam Potter's got on the NSC staff, and he's been skulking around Washington without anybody knowing about it. There's been a deal cooking to back that so-called revolution of his, and he's apparently convinced everybody, including my daughter, that he's the great hope of the people."

Clayton felt a prickling on the back of his neck and tried not to tighten his comforting clasp of Tracy's hand.

"What's all this about a deal?" He tried not to sound too intense.

"Charley Dill says Sam's lost his marbles if he thinks he can pull something like this off in an election year just because Billy the Kid's convinced him Filega can bring democracy to Central America. Charley says Sam doesn't know Jared and he's right. I know Jared and he was power crazy even in law school. He loves violence, too. Always did. Even in bed."

Tracy blew her nose while Clayton tried to absorb what she had so casually dropped in his lap. He would have to check it out, of course, but what she was saying was that she'd been told by the co-chairman of the Joint Committee on Intelligence that the President of the United States was involved in a clandestine deal with a Central American revolutionary of dubious reputation and reliability. There had been grumblings and rumblings among Capitol Hill liberals about presidential bad judgment in even meeting with Filega during a Central American summit. This meant Potter had accepted the judgment of a conservative young army officer working as an aide to the National Security Council that Filega could be trusted. If what Tracy said was true, Clayton had witnessed the hatching of a golden egg. All these years, he'd been right about her, and as it turned out, a little human sympathy was the key. She was starved for someone to listen to *her*. He felt like hugging her, but contented himself with patting her hand.

Clayton also knew he had to tread carefully.

"What you're talking about," he said, "well, there's been a lot of talk about it around town, of course"—that was a lie—"and I've been sort of sitting on it as a story." He stole a glance at her to measure her reaction, but Tracy was nodding affirmation.

"That's what Charley warned Sam—that it'd get out, and there would be real trouble in an election year. I'm not surprised you know, Clayton."

She sighed, and her thoughts obviously were far from Filega and foreign policy. Clayton considered his strategy.

"You know, Tracy, I'm impressed by your knowledge of this. You've known about it all along, and I'll bet there's a lot of stuff that's tucked away in your head that you don't talk about. It's remarkable."

Tracy laughed nervously.

"Well, after all, Clayton, these people are friends of mine. I've known them for ages and they trust me," she said. "Although, as you say, it usually does come out. Not all of it, though!" Her eyes sparkled suddenly, and Clayton felt a responsive tingle.

"I'm sure of that." He smiled at her encouragingly and she smiled back.

"Well, poor dear Clayton, I'm so sorry I put you through this." She opened her menu again. "I'll get over it—I don't have much choice, I guess—and we can go back to having fun lunches again. It all got to me, I think, and I realized I'd nobody to talk to."

"But you do, Tracy. You have me."

She looked at him over the menu. "Well, I'm not going to go on boring you about Tommy and his boyfriend or my daughter and her revolutionary lover."

Clayton ordered another glass of wine and was pleased she did not offer her usual objection. "We," he announced, "are celebrating a new day in our friendship. As of today, we can tell each other anything. If I'm depressed, I can tell you, and if you're depressed, you'll tell me. We'll talk about what's going on in our lives." He looked solemn. "I know what it is to go through a marriage split myself."

Tracy stroked his hand. "I know you do. That was sad about you and Barbie."

It was typical of Tracy, he thought, that she would remember the name of a woman he hadn't seen for several years and never spoke about.

"But you don't want to hear chitchat, Clayton. I mean, you tell such interesting stories about your work, and I enjoy hearing about it. Most of what I hear is just gossip from parties and dinners, and you know how dull that can be."

"I'd be willing to bet," he said sincerely, "that I'd be *just* as fascinated by your anecdotes as you are by newspaper stories. Just different brands of gossip, really. And you see, what you hear, Tracy, is often the link in the chain. As you've just demonstrated today."

She was listening. There was curiosity in her face. Then she shook her head at him.

"Clayton, come on. I'm no source for you. You know I've never done that. I'm not going to have people think I leak to the press."

"I'm not suggesting such a thing. I know how loyal a friend you are. All the years we've been having lunch together, what have you leaked?"

"Nothing that I know of."

"Right. I don't want you to betray anybody. What I'm saying is you should talk about *yourself,* Tracy. And I'm quite certain a lot of people would be interested."

"In me? Why?"

"Because—because you're sort of a Washington social historian. You've been here for what—twenty years?—and you're part of the establishment. You've seen administrations come and go and known why. You know the people who used to be in as well as the ones who are in."

"Perhaps. But, Clayton, I keep telling you, I'm no source for stories."

Clayton looked into her eyes earnestly and made what he had decided was the only pitch that might work. "Not for stories. For a book."

Tracy stared at him. "A book? You're joking. What about?"

"About you."

She laughed and went back to scanning the menu. "Clayton, you're an old flatterer. I don't even write letters to my mother, so it's unlikely I'd write a book."

"Well"—he hesitated before plunging on—"you'd probably need some help with the writing. But you'd have me for that. If you wanted me, of course."

"You're serious about this? You're crazy!"

"I'm not." He leaned forward.

"If I can't persuade you, would you listen to an editor from a New York publishing house who's a friend of mine and who happens to be looking for people who are authorities on Washington?"

"Come on, Clayton." Tracy looked up at the waiter and smiled at him. "I'll have the crab salad, please."

"Crab crepes," said Clayton, "and another glass of wine."

"Not for me. My heavens." Tracy shook her head and, as the waiter left, took out a tiny mirror and searched for signs of wear and tear from her weeping. She fluffed her silvery bangs, put the mirror back in her purse, and smiled at Clayton.

"You're being very sweet and I appreciate it. But you don't have to go this far." She giggled. "Can you imagine me writing a book? What's even more unlikely, can you imagine anybody reading it? Cocktail parties I have attended. What to do about the blisters you get on your feet from standing and on your mind from boredom. Soirees that have given me indigestion. Dinner partners who have sent me to sleep. Beds I have bounced on!" She burst into laughter.

Clayton nodded, not discouraged by her frivolous response.

"That's exactly what I can imagine. People are fascinated by what goes on in Washington, Tracy, and not just the big picture. The little things, the details. You have an unusual perspective, especially as you have a sense of humor about it all. You could write a social chronicle, full of little human touches."

Tracy contemplated her still half-full glass of wine.

"It's too unlikely," she said, but there was uncertainty in her voice, a wavering of her previous tone of dismissal.

"Listen. Will you at least let me introduce you to this editor friend of mine? He's going to be down for the weekend anyway. It couldn't hurt to talk to him, could it? And it'd take your mind off Tommy and Rosemarie, wouldn't it? What you need, Tracy, is a new interest. You need to take care of yourself. You don't appreciate yourself. Look at the biographies written by all kinds of people who've lived here, politicians, commentators, lobbyists, probably none of them with any more insight than you have. And some of those books were best-sellers. They made money."

Her eyes sharpened, and Clayton pressed on.

"Tracy, as an old friend, let me ask you. Did Tommy leave you well off? Aren't you going to have to think about money?"

She nodded, and dabbed at her eyes again.

"Then this is the ideal time for you to at least think about this kind of project. Suppose this editor was interested enough to offer you advance for an outline of a book? You tell him what you'd write about and he'd decide whether they would want to make an offer. That'd be a help, wouldn't it?"

"Well, yes, it would. I could certainly use the money. But I still can't believe anyone would be interested in anything I had to say, Clayton."

"Tell you what. Why don't you let Jerry—that's my friend—be the judge of that. We'll have a chat over at my house, just the three of us. You can reminisce a little bit about the changes you've seen in Washington—the style of the city, the parties, the people, the White House. I'm sure you can remember interesting stories about old political deals struck at parties, funny stories about mishaps nobody ever heard of, your own impressions of people everyone's heard of and don't know as well as you do. . . ."

Tracy was staring at her salad.

"Why not?" he asked.

She picked up her fork. "I don't feel quite right about it. I mean, I don't want to hurt anybody, Clayton. I don't like to upset people."

"My dear, I know that. Everybody knows that. You're too

kindhearted to hurt anybody. But this kind of thing would make people laugh! And anyway, think of this. Aren't you the one who's always giving, taking care of people, listening to them? I mean, who's taking care of *you* now that you need somebody?"

She put down her fork and looked at him, lips pursed. Clayton's heart rose.

"Maybe you have a point," she said cautiously. "It's true people kind of lean on me—not that I mind, of course."

"Of course not. But how often do they call when they don't need you?"

Her face shadowed. "Well, I get invited out a lot, and people are nice to me—"

"Which isn't surprising, since you're probably the saving grace of a lot of dull dinner parties."

Tracy smiled. "Clayton, you are a dear. You've been so good for me today. I can't tell you how much better I feel!"

"This is just the beginning," he said. "You're going to feel even better because you're going to be somebody in your own right. Not just Tracy the party girl." That struck home.

"You know," said Tracy, "Tommy—when he told me he was leaving—he said something about my being always so—so damned agreeable was how I think he put it. He said people called me Tracy the soft touch. Have you ever heard that?"

Clayton was familiar with the nickname, which was widely used. But he shook his head firmly.

"I've never heard that, and frankly, I don't want to criticize Tommy, but I'm disappointed in him. It's not just the Raymond business, but he's behaved badly. He's not only abandoned you without any warning, but he's left you in a real financial bind, Tracy. He didn't have to be this rough with you."

He knew there were many who would have assumed Tracy would barely notice Tommy's absence. But he wanted above all to establish in her mind who her real friends were. Or who her real *friend* was. Clayton was not about to let a talking Tracy escape him. He was determined that by the time they left the restaurant, he would be Tracy's best friend. Only in that role could he accomplish the journalistic goals that suddenly shone ahead of him.

Tracy dabbed at her eyes again with his handkerchief, realized what she was using, and smiled appreciatively as she handed it back to him.

"I'll still think you've lost your mind, Clayton, but if you really are serious about this, I'll come talk to you and your editor friend."

"Wonderful," said Clayton. "How about Friday? I make a great bouillabaisse."

"I don't think I can," said Tracy, searching for her engagement diary.

"How about next Thursday?"

"Tracy," said Clayton, alarmed at the suggestion of a delay that would give her a chance to change her mind, "what are you doing that's more important than this? What's more important than talking about a book that could help you out financially? Maybe make you a lot of money? You have to take this seriously or the editor won't."

She hesitated. "I suppose I could cancel . . ."

"Of course you could. Then it's set. Dinner Friday at my house."

"You're managing me," she said coquettishly.

"I'm rescuing you," he told her. Tracy was silent, looking thoughtful. Then he was relieved to see an expression of determination on her face.

"Maybe you're right," she said. "When I think of some of the silly books I've read about Washington, and some of those book parties, well, maybe I might have something to say. But you'd have to help me. It'd take up a lot of your time.

Clayton reached across the table and shook her hand. "Tracy, you can count on me."

Chapter Five

"Who leaked it?" demanded President Samuel Perkins Potter, throwing on his desk a clipping of a story by Clayton Clapper in which the administration was accused of making a clandestine deal with a Central American revolutionary dedicated to overthrowing a government that had the backing of liberals on Capitol Hill.

"I know who it was," the President continued, before either Secretary of State Ford Gibson or White House Press Secretary Jim Dibble could open his mouth.

"That bastard Charley Dill. He's been snapping at my heels since North Carolina lost those bases and didn't get that laser contract."

No disagreement was offered, because both men were aware of the futility of trying to interrupt Potter in full tirade. For one thing, he didn't listen to anything except his own reverberating voice at such moments. The solution was to wait until he wore himself out, then offer an opinion marginally different from his in order to get his attention. After that it became possible to disagree with him.

"Charley's been complaining in private we owed him one and we hadn't come through," Gibson acknowledged cautiously. "But he's tight-mouthed. This isn't how he goes about things. It's too heavy-handed, too obvious. He'd have back-doored it."

"However he goes about things, it's the same damned result," snarled the President. "We're going to have the press braying for investigations and special prosecutors and congressional hearings in the middle of a goddamned election year."

"But that's the point. This won't do Dill any good, either. That's what I don't understand," said Dibble. "I mean, he's up, too, this year, and his hands aren't all that clean. And he knows we know it."

"You mean that business in the Middle East last year when we finally took care of that bastard? That's true, Charley was helpful about that," agreed Gibson. "That's why he was in an uproar about the contract."

"If not Dill, then who?" asked the President, poking peevishly at his leather desk blotter with a gold paper knife embossed with the presidential seal.

"Clapper's never come up with anything this tough before in a column. His stuff's usually more catch-up, more hysterical, not the sledgehammer. He's got himself some new sources," said Dibble, chewing on his lower lip.

"What about Rob Klinger in Dill's office? He's tight with some of the press," the press secretary suggested.

"Klinger knows better. Charley'd skin him. He'd never get another job as good on the Hill. What worries me is this damned thing is pretty accurate, and there aren't that many people who could have been this close on it." The presidential voice was rising again, and Gibson and Dibble sighed.

The President picked up the phone. "Get me Senator Dill," he ordered, ignoring the uneasy fidgeting on the other side of his desk.

"Maybe we ought to discuss this more, Mr. President." Gibson was recalling a previous occasion when an enraged

Potter, who hadn't been dubbed the mad dog of the Senate for nothing, threatened to bash in the head of a politically perfidious senator.

Potter paid no attention.

"Charley?" he said after a moment, "You seen that Clapper piece this morning? Yeah. Where in the hell—" He paused and listened, which was unusual under such circumstances. Dibble and Gibson exchanged curious glances. After a few moments, the presidential expression lost some of its belligerence.

"Goddamn," he said mildly. "See what you mean. Yeah, let me know."

He hung up.

"He's madder'n I am," he said in a tone combining relief with disbelief.

"He have any ideas on where Clapper got it?"

Potter shook his head. "Insists it was nobody in his shop. For one thing, nobody but him knew about Todd. He's sweating it."

"You believe him?"

Potter pushed his hands through his shock of white hair.

"Yes," he said finally. "Charley's got too much to lose. He's too long in the political tooth to make this kind of play." He looked at the secretary of state. "You're right, Ford," he said. "It doesn't make sense, because both sides of the aisle are involved, especially when you take the Middle East thing into account. Charley can't afford to have that leaked. But he's been shooting his mouth off about irresponsibility in foreign policy at the White House to mollify the liberals, and now the whole damned press assumes he's behind this."

"I have a press briefing coming up," Dibble said morosely.

"Got any raw meat you can throw 'em?" the President asked.

"Your boy Toady—I mean Todd," said Dibble, whose

outspokenness was both cherished and denounced by the President. Potter's head came up sharply at the reference to Col. Todd William Neville, a National Security Council aide referred to as Billy the Kid because of his readiness to launch maverick missions for his country without counting the cost politically, professionally, or diplomatically.

"Watch your mouth, Jim," said Potter. "We know it wasn't Todd who leaked. Fine young man. True patriot."

Ford Gibson squirmed in his chair. He found it difficult to understand why an otherwise astute politician like Potter was afflicted by what his staff referred to privately as his John Wayne heel.

"The point is, Mr. President," Gibson said, "they're going to go after Colonel Neville next. We don't know what else Clapper's got. That column does mention the NSC and its cowboys, as he calls them. He's going to parlay it as long as possible and everybody else will jump on the bandwagon."

Potter looked sullen. "I know what you're getting at, Ford," he said. "But I still think I'm right about Filega. He's a tough bastard, but he gets things done."

"We've discussed his methods before," Gibson retorted stiffly.

"We could get Neville out of town for a while," Potter said.

Dibble rolled his eyes. "He's been out of town for a while. That's the trouble."

"Goddamnit," said Potter. "You people will eat your words about him one of these days."

The two men were silent as he glared at them. When Dibble spoke, his voice was weary.

"This town loves a good juicy scandal and it hasn't had one for a while. Not only that, but the press has been grumbling about a dull election year, because you're expected to win, sir," he said. Potter digested that for a while.

"We could . . . put things on hold with Filega until this blows over," he offered.

"If it blows over," said Gibson.

"Oh, Jesus," said Potter.

"What about the briefing?" Dibble asked.

"Hedge a denial," said Potter.

Dibble's sigh almost blew him out of the Oval Office.

"We're going to have to hang in there for a day or two, see what happens. Sometimes these things die down," Potter said without conviction. He'd seen this kind of thing before, and they all knew it. They also knew what could be ahead.

"Where in hell did Clapper get it?" Potter muttered as Dibble and Gibson turned toward the door. Gibson was aware of a certain relief. He did not underestimate the potential political fallout, but he also wondered whether Clapper's column might have saved the administration from itself.

Sam Potter was a popular President partly because he knew how to run with political issues, partly because he convinced millions of upwardly mobile middle-class Americans it was not only healthy, but mandatory to believe in a Norman Rockwell image of America the beautiful, land of lighted windows, quiet tree-lined streets, and happy families. He never explained how drug wars, street crime, homelessness, and pollution fitted into the idyll. But the polls made clear that voters were willing to gulp down the psychological placebos dished out by the White House in masterfully genial television appearances. Potter's weakness was his concept of himself as a diplomatic crusader whose sights were still set on the lessons learned from the mistakes of World War II and what he considered the weak leadership that had made Vietnam such a costly error in judgment.

He believed, he was fond of saying, in cutting through to the root of a problem with whatever force might be necessary. Potter tended to be a patsy for the Pentagon's insistence on the need for weapons despite the outbreak of peace in parts of the world which once had bolstered that argument.

He fought an endless battle with opponents on Capitol Hill who denounced him for espousing policies they considered three decades out of date. Those were the senators and congressmen who would greet Clayton Clapper's column with whoops of glee and calls for a full-scale congressional inquiry, complete with televised hearings at which administration witnesses could be held up to ridicule.

Senator Charley Dill was as aware of what lay ahead as President Potter. He had taken Potter's call while having a cup of coffee—laced with a splash of brandy to sooth nerves frazzled by press calls—in his private office with his friend and colleague Senator Eleanor McClusky of Illinois. She was sympathetic, yet puzzled, because she hadn't been aware of many of the points mentioned in the Clapper story, and she had discovered that Dill had been.

"You mean the Clapper stuff is all accurate?" she asked, sipping coffee unembellished by brandy.

Dill looked a little uncomfortable. "Well, in essence, Eleanor. In essence."

"That means he was right. You knew what Sam was up to with Filega?"

The reproach in her voice didn't pass unnoticed by Dill.

"I've been trying to get him to back off, but he's got the Lone Ranger or whatever they call that mad colonel on the NSC egging him on, and you know what—"

"Sam's like." She finished his sentence.

"But I'm still surprised," she said. "Especially with an election campaign on. He's given them a real gift of an issue."

"Don't I know it. Puts me on the hot seat as well. Everybody thinks I leaked it."

"You can go on the record opposing administration contacts with Filega, Charley. You've already spoken out about it. That's no secret."

"I can." The unspoken "but" hung in the air. She waited, but Dill maintained a gloomy silence.

"Charley," said Eleanor, "what else is going on?"

He stared at her. "What d'you mean?"

"Just wondered."

He took a gulp of coffee. "Don't be so suspicious, Eleanor."

She hesitated, then changed the subject. Charley would tell her only when he wanted to tell her. "You know Clapper?"

He nodded. "He's been around awhile and he's conscientious and hardworking, but he doesn't usually lead the pack with this kind of thing. I'd give a lot to know where he got this stuff."

"You think this isn't the end of it?"

"Hell, no. He's bound to be saving some for a follow-up. And presumably he'll go back to the source for more of the same."

"What else is there?"

"Damned if I know, Eleanor. I try to take this life one day at a time, and I could do without this one."

Eleanor sighed. "Well, I'd better get back to my office. See you at the committee meeting this afternoon."

He nodded distractedly, and she left with a feeling of dissatisfaction mixed with resentment that Charley Dill's friendship apparently didn't extend to trusting her. She knew Charley didn't tell her everything, and she didn't expect him to. But this was different. She knew he wasn't involved in the Filega business, so what was it? She supposed she'd find out, and she had a feeling she wasn't going to like it. She found a stack of messages awaiting her in her office, where her press secretary, Joan Utter, was pulling a face and waving simultaneously as she came in.

"Your uncle's on the line again."

Eleanor heaved an exaggerated sigh and went into her private office, where she picked up the telephone with the reluctance that always accompanied her conversations with Francis Sikorski. Partly because she had reason to believe his line was bugged by the FBI.

"Uncle Francis," she said.

"Ellie, my dear." He was the only person in the world who called her Ellie. He bragged about how proud he was of his niece who was a United States senator, although he was related to Eleanor only because her father's sister had divorced what her family considered a perfectly respectable husband to marry a man widely believed to be the godfather of a Mafia family in Chicago. It made Eleanor nervous when Sikorski mentioned blood being thicker than water. He didn't care whether the rest of the McCluskys ostracized him, but he was determined to cultivate the friendship of a lawmaker. Eleanor had made clear theirs was a tenuous affinity, but he knew she was fond of her Aunt Polly, and he was convinced someday she would need him. In his world, somebody always needed something or somebody sooner or later.

So he kept in touch, although her distant manner grated on him. He was accustomed to women who knew their place.

"I hadn't heard from you in so long, we got worried about you," he told her, his harsh voice mellowed to an unctuous growl. "Your aunt was just asking why don't we ever see Ellie any more, and I said, well, I'd ask her to have dinner with us next time she's out seeing her constituents."

"How lovely," said Eleanor.

"Then I said to myself, why wait that long? You're always so booked up when you're here, you never have a minute for us old folks. So why don't we go and see her ourselves, I said to Polly. We can have dinner in Washington, just family. Just the three of us."

"How nice," said Eleanor.

"So we're coming to Washington, Polly and me. Just to see you, Ellie. Give you a night out."

"When?"

"Next week."

"Oh, that's—I'm afraid that's when things are really busy, Uncle Francis." Eleanor looked wildly at Joan Utter, who was leaning against the door, shaking her head in sympathy.

"Well, the week after. You're not putting us off this time, Ellie. We're comin' up if we have to camp out on your doorstep up there on Capitol Hill."

Eleanor shuddered.

"Well, maybe next Wednesday," she said in a tone like the tolling of a bell.

"Next Wednesday it is! You pick the place. One of those fancy restaurants where we can see all your friends. Only the best, Ellie."

Eleanor made a mental note to get reservations in the darkest corner of a restaurant in farthest Bethesda.

"How's Aunt Polly?" she asked.

"Great, great. She's dyin' to see you."

Eleanor shivered. "I'll look forward to it, Uncle Francis."

She put down the phone and put her head in her hands. Joan Utter touched her lightly on the shoulder.

"No way out?"

Eleanor shook her head.

"How long has it been since you've seen him?"

"About two years."

"I think you can risk a biennial dinner without political disaster. Why not have other relatives along—dilute the impact?"

"They wouldn't be caught dead with him in public. And I do like Aunt Polly. It hurts her feelings that I don't see her. She's a nice woman, just dizzy. She says he's wonderful to her. Always buying her expensive presents."

"She knows about him, doesn't she?"

"Aunt Polly doesn't let herself think about things like that. It disturbs the even tenor of her days."

Jean laughed. "I could come along," she offered. "I kind of enjoy the old monster. He keeps trying to imitate Marlon Brando, and it's funnier than he realizes."

Eleanor smiled weakly and shook her head. "Thanks, but no. I have a feeling it's not an imitation, and your presence might make it look like official business instead of an awkward family gathering."

"Well, your aunt'll be there. That should help."

"She's a dear, but she never gets a word in edgewise. The worst of it is, she dotes on every word he says."

"That's probably what appeals to him about her."

Eleanor nodded and sighed. Usually she welcomed a visit from old friends. She was lonelier than she admitted, even to herself. She had dedicated herself to her career. That was all that mattered to her since the night before her wedding seven years ago when her fiance decided that they weren't right for each other. The knowledge that he was right hadn't eased the bruise to her pride, and she'd taken malicious satisfaction in his failure in a run for local office the same year she'd been elected in a tough fight for a U.S. Senate seat.

She'd done well in her first term and expected little problem in her forthcoming reelection campaign. But she lived a solitary life, and it wasn't because she was a social failure in Washington. The elegant, charming Senator McClusky was in demand. But she always went home alone to the quiet apartment with its high-ceilinged rooms full of antiques and its windows overlooking the city.

She'd never taken a man home with her because she hadn't wanted to. That was something else she'd come to terms with, over recent years. Eleanor had many friends in Washington, but none of them knew her well. Even her staff, with whom she was popular, admitted she could be remote. She would talk politics or art by the hour, with easy enthusiasm, but her personal life was locked and shuttered.

"I don't think she *has* a personal life," Joan Utter observed to another staff member. "I think politics is her life."

That was true only up to a point. Eleanor was not only solitary, she was lonely, but it was well concealed, and because she was so busy most of the time, she didn't realize herself how isolated she had become. Achieving satisfaction by revenging herself on the man who had abandoned her had long evaporated. It had been replaced by a deep sadness and a conviction that she would not and could not find the kind of traditional happiness she once took for granted.

She had never risked rejection again. Now it was she who called the turn, and she made choices according to personal whim because none of them mattered. Her looks, intelligence, and charm ensured her control and also her popularity. But she still went home alone. Except for one rainy night after a dinner party when she had invited a fellow guest to have an afterdinner drink at her apartment.

She had talked for the first time in years, telling things about herself, confessing vulnerabilities, even laughing over them. Far into the night she had talked, captured by warm, understanding eyes and slender hands that occasionally patted in consolation yet made no demands.

That was the night she had discovered a surprising joy. She had been both happy and uneasy, aware of the precipice on which she stood. She had never forgotten it. The memory of that night still comforted her. It also frightened her.

Chapter Six

A new world had opened for Tracy, and it didn't hurt that its door was held ajar by Jerry Kennally, editor in chief of Wissip Golight, an old publishing house newly acquired by Robert Mortimer, a multimillionaire who had made his money in overpriced real estate and was now hell-bent on buying himself social entrée. As a means of invading what he considered the world of the cultivated, Mortimer bought for a substantial sum the 150-year-old establishment founded by William Wissip and George Golight in an era when the Brontë sisters were considered daring.

WG had a reputation for printing nothing that you wouldn't want your mother to read, but the publishing house also knew how to give readers what, in the old days, they wanted, as well as what was good for them. The firm turned a nice profit until it was seduced by the sexual revolution and its readership underwent a metamorphosis of taste that left the few vulnerable publishers floundering as the reading public drifted steadily from the prudent to the prurient. When Old Mr. W., as he was known throughout the business, died, some said it was attributable to his being offered a manuscript that dealt in graphic detail, not only with the usual vices, but with innovative deviations from them.

WG was ripe for a coup, and Robert Mortimer was waiting. Mortimer, a dapper, tough little man who looked like a well-tailored mouse, made it clear from the outset that he wanted value for his money, as well as a ticket to literary cocktail parties.

He wanted the kind of profits WG had never dreamed of in its golden years. He sought authors who commanded bookings on talk shows and in gossip columns as well as attention in the *New York Times Book Review.* For such books, he was prepared to spend money, especially since he could write a good deal of it off. He took risks in order to capture public attention, on the theory that dabbling in acceptable scandal was good for sales. Washington fascinated Mortimer, because he was a classic case of arriviste ambition, combined with recurrent visions of himself as a viable political candidate. This explained why he took elocution lessons to improve a shrill voice and a New York accent.

Mortimer wanted big Washington books of the sort Bob Woodward wrote, but a lot juicier. He warned his editors he did not want tomes by heavy thinkers analyzing sociological trends, prompting ponderous reviews, because such books had zero appeal to the mass market. He wanted books that told people what those fuckers in Washington were really up to, as he put it, because he was convinced they were the fast track to best-sellerdom.

A veteran editor at WG, who suggested that Mortimer should have bought a supermarket tabloid instead of a respectable publishing company, was advised to take early retirement. Mortimer wanted people who measured up to his personal standards of prurient excellence.

He decided the firm would continue to be known as Wissip Golight because it carried a certain cachet in publishing, whereas the Mortimer name was still associated with construction and the kind of buildings that offended everyone who did not associate architecture with towering triangles of marble and glass. The editor who had been involuntarily retired left a note on the bulletin board suggesting that what WG now stood for was Wild and Gaudy. Mortimer's small mouth widened in a faint smile when he read it; he did not entirely dispute the editor's description. He proceeded to hire editors from other firms, paying them huge salaries calculated to remind them continually of the kinds of books they were expected to acquire. Some of his editors came from newspapers that never let truth stand in the way of a good story. This was precisely what Mortimer wanted: editors who were smart enough to know where to draw the line at libel, and hardheaded enough to be unimpeded by scruples.

A member of that breed was Mortimer's editor in chief, Jerry Kennally, a tweedy transplant from London's Fleet Street, whose career had since taken him to newspapers in Washington and New York, where a hired gun could command a high salary. He had gone to work for a publishing company looking for someone who could troll the Washington market for controversy, conspiracy, and shenanigans.

Kennally, who respected Mortimer's money but despised the man, a not unusual reaction on his part, was a tall, self-assured man with a lopsided grin and a faintly professorial look, achieved by training a lock of thick dark hair to flop over his forehead. He spoke with an accent that made him sound much better educated than he was, a style that Mortimer envied. Most important, he offered no arguments about the importance of educating the reading public by publishing books of literary merit. Kennally just wanted to make money and have a good time doing it; putting up with the likes of Mortimer left him unruffled and faintly amused. Mortimer and Kennally could use each other, and in their own way, each recognized it and was comfortable with it.

With Mortimer's blessing, Kennally settled into one of the most expensive hotels in Washington to winnow out some promising books or make contacts who could lead him to books. One of those contacts was Clayton Clapper, whom Kennally had known during one of his Washington stints. He had come to respect Clayton. He also recognized that Clayton was getting more anxious for a journalistic coup that would crown his efforts and gain recognition on the national level. Looking at Clayton, Kennally noted the nervously tapping fingers, the expanding waistline, and the watery, worried brown eyes in a florid face. Clayton was desperate. He was manna for Mortimer. When Clayton told him about Tracy Gilmartin, Kennally was cautious, but interested. He knew unlikely sources could be astonishingly rewarding, and he gathered Tracy was an untapped source. He could only hope it wouldn't be plumbing a puddle. When he met Tracy, his doubts deepened. He decided he'd like to go to bed with her, but he wasn't sure he'd want to publish her. Yet he had a lot of faith in Clayton Clapper.

After spending a few hours with Tracy, Kennally still had reservations about how to tailor what he dubbed "Tracy-talk" into a manageable manuscript. He thought he'd rarely met anyone with so little to say and so much to talk about. He actually found himself talking to *her* at first, while she listened and Clayton smiled smugly.

Clayton had been smiling a lot since his story on Jared Filega had aroused such a satisfying furor. It had sent his journalistic stock up sharply. He'd been able to follow up with stories on congressional demands for investigation and denunciations from the left, and his patient questioning of Tracy had elicited the additional tidbit that the administration was backing off on its Central American ploy as a matter of political expediency.

Clayton was more than pleased with the results of persuading Tracy to confide in him. He watched without surprise as Kennally went through the same doubts and confusion evoked by Tracy's manner, which was sweet but vague, and her chocolate-box appearance. At first she was wary of Kennally, although she was comforted by his high-voltage charm and assurances of WG's abiding interest in the social history of the nation's capital.

"We do want it to be lighthearted, of course," Kennally explained. "Lots of funny anecdotes to illustrate reaction to events, and, of course, with your own observations.

"Perhaps you should think about sitting down with Clayton and letting him take notes, or tape you. Just reminisce about your life here, all the interesting people you've known and what it was like when things were really popping politically at times like Watergate and Vietnam.

"Your little personal touches are so important because they give texture to your memory. For example, you may recall a particularly astute or interesting comment made by a congressman or cabinet officer at an important time. On a more personal level, perhaps the strain imposed by Washington life on the marriage of one of your friends in a powerful position."

Kennally paused in his application of soothing syrup as Tracy laughed.

"You mean marriages, plural! Countless! I remember one time talking and talking with David McCord when he was Vice President and he told me his marriage was in shreds because Jeanne had this longtime thing going with Dick Gilt, the political columnist. They'd have these huge fights, with things flying about, and once the neighbors actually complained about the noise and of course they had to say it was the stereo volume out of whack. Then poor David would get hell from the President for not being able to control his domestic life and I was just so sorry for him. I remember one day it was so hot and we sort of wound up taking a shower together, or not quite together, but sort of, and he said he hoped he wouldn't get the nomination because what he really wanted to do was run away with me. I don't mean to sound conceited but he was so unhappy and he was really such a dear . . ."

Tracy looked nostalgic. Kennally looked at her with bright, interested eyes.

"I can absolutely understand anyone wanting to run away with you, Tracy," he told her. He looked deep into her eyes and she giggled.

"Well, you see what I mean," she said. "It's just little things like that that I remember."

"But that's absolutely fascinating!" Kennally said with genuine sincerity.

"You just told us a political anecdote that I'd never heard before. I mean, that McCord's failure to win the nomination four years ago was partly due to his problems at home. Sounds as though he'd have got a big sympathy vote!"

He grinned engagingly and Tracy nodded.

"That's absolutely true. Dick kept sniping at poor David in his columns, and of course he had all this inside stuff because he got it in bed from Jeanne and poor David never knew *what* he'd wake up and read in the morning papers. Everybody kept saying Dick had such great sources because nobody, practically, knew who the source was and nobody ever found out. I was so terribly sorry for David."

"Didn't Gilt get married to a television reporter quite recently?" asked Clayton.

"That was the worst part," said Tracy sorrowfully. "After it was all over and poor David was done for politically, Jeanne walked out on him and went straight to Dick, and guess what?"

"I can guess," said Kennally.

"Well, I felt a little bit sorry for Jeanne over that. She really could be the most charming woman, and she was nice, except to poor David, and she was really just crushed about Dick, but he was simply using her, of course. She was just broken up about it, especially as she said she might have been First Lady if she hadn't screwed David because she wanted so badly to screw Dick, and then Dick was so cold, she couldn't believe it. She said to me one time at lunch it was just as though Dick were a stranger all of a sudden and then all David wanted was a divorce. Anyway, he was the one with all the money, so he went on a cruise and met Jenny Ruxton, the rock singer who went into opera, you remember? She was the love of his life, but he told me when he got back and then *they* broke up that he couldn't deal with a woman who wanted to make love in galoshes."

Tracy's laugh rippled.

"Galoshes?" Kennally smiled at her in a manner that suggested they were already closer than two people who had just met. Tracy laughed again. It was fortunate, Kennally thought, that she had a husky, pretty laugh, because you certainly heard a lot of it.

"Oh, *God,* the most unlikely people do the most *unlikely* things," she gurgled. "I mean, when Sam told me he liked to be spanked first, I just about died."

Clayton didn't open his mouth to ask a question in case she stopped talking, but contented himself with watching Kennally's expression.

"I mean, it *was* a long time ago, but I don't think he's changed any. In fact, I *know* he hasn't! But he and I were very good friends when he was in the Senate, and, well, everybody's kinky one way or another, aren't they? What's really funny is so is Vladimir."

"Vladimir," Clayton repeated in a hushed voice.

Tracy smiled at him angelically. "Oh, God, yes. It's always struck me as just hilarious they have this little funny thing in common and of course they don't know it. I mean, they ought to get along, oughtn't they?"

"Indeed they ought," Kennally agreed. His eyes had taken on a mad gleam.

Tracy sighed and sipped a little wine. Clayton had

warned Kennally against trying to get her drunk, pointing out that she was sufficiently discombobulated in conversation when sober and liquor would make her sound like a garbled tape.

"How do you plan to turn her reminiscences into a manuscript?" Kennally asked when Tracy briefly left the room.

"Very carefully," said Clayton. "The stuff's there, as you can tell. It's a matter of collating what's in her mind. It's true, up to a point, that she doesn't realize how much she knows. What's fascinating is the way she can take off on one point and keep expanding in all directions. I think disciplining her and pinning her down will be the most difficult job."

"Obviously," said Kennally. "Some of her inside stuff is vastly entertaining, but it may be touchy to get it into print. Was that the President she was talking about? Spanking?"

Clayton exploded into laughter. "When she talks about Sam, she means the President. It's risky to ask her *who* she's talking about because then she worries she's letting her friends down."

"And Vladimir?"

"I assume that's the Soviet ambassador."

Kennally chuckled. "That's goddamned wonderful. S and M in the White House and the Russian embassy! They could be happy spanking the hell out of each other while negotiating arms control. If they only knew!"

Clayton wiped his eyes. "What we have to do, as I see it, is get her back as far as she can remember, get it all on paper, then whip it into shape."

"Meantime, we can plant some teasers in newspaper columns, especially since there may be some stories the lawyers won't let us use. We can dribble some anecdotes out and drive everybody wild."

"Absolutely. Once she gets comfortable with the idea, I think we can move fast. She's still surprised anybody wants to listen to what she has to say. And she's still concerned about being indiscreet."

"Why is that such a problem with her? I mean, she's likely to make a lot of money with this book. Christ, it'll be like a gigantic gossip column. Twenty years of tittle-tattle. People eat that kind of stuff up like junk food."

"These really are her friends. She doesn't like to hurt people. She's not malicious at all. She's goofy, but she's gentle."

Kennally shook his head. "Bambi in the jungle of Washington."

"Anyway, you do agree with me about her credentials?"

"Christ, yes, Mortimer'll love it. He wants to make a splash that'll get him noticed in the kind of circles he'd like to move in, God knows why, and first he has to get attention outside the banking and lumber business. But I tell you, Clayton, you're going to have to nail her down. How do you do that? We're relying on her memory? Isn't that chancy?"

Clayton poured himself another drink and frowned. "I've been thinking about that, too, especially because she's so disorganized. And I wondered . . ."

They both looked up as Tracy came back into Clayton's living room, to which they had retreated after dinner.

"Clayton, such a darling bathroom. Purple!" she chirped.

"That was the previous owners," he said uncomfortably. "I find purple first thing in the morning almost more than I can face."

"So dramatic," said Tracy. "You know, I always find it interesting, the colors people can live with. We're—I mean I'm conventional, really. Chintz and leather, that kind of thing. Tommy liked it and I didn't really care. But I remember how fascinated I was when I went to dinner at Saul Horwitz's house and everything was white except the bathroom. That was black. I know he's made a lot of money off those books about how to control your darker impulses. I mean, all that stuff about what to do *instead* of killing your boss or your wife. But I kept thinking how difficult it must be to keep white really white and not that awful dingy white, with those little splotches where you almost got a stain off, but not quite."

"You know Horwitz well?" Kennally asked.

Saul Horwitz was a reclusive author. He hadn't given a newspaper or magazine interview in fifteen years. He had a clause in his contract specifying he would not have to tolerate intrusion. He was equally firm about the size of advances he considered suitable for his next four hundred-page advisory on how not to lose one's temper. That was, as one critic put it, what *all* of his books were about, snapped up by an eager market. All Horwitz books were best-sellers, and Kennally never argued with success.

"Not *very* well," said Tracy. "But he did invite me to lunch after I met him. He's really quite a nice man. Sort of shy. And he is obsessed with color. Said he started writing his books after he had his colors done in California and this woman told him he could only produce in a virginal environment. I guess that's the reason for the white house."

She laughed again.

"It was sort of like sitting in a snowdrift. He flinched because I was wearing a red dress. He said it made him think of blood and he couldn't eat, so I offered to go home and change but he brought me one of his white shirts to put over my dress instead and we had a nice lunch."

"White?" Kennally inquired.

"As a matter of fact. Chicken breast. Water chestnuts. Vanilla ice cream. And milk. In wineglasses."

"You've been to a lot of White House affairs, haven't you?" Kennally asked. He reflected he might have phrased the question more subtly.

"Yes, three administrations' worth of them. I mean, once you sort of get accepted at a certain level in Washington and you don't tread on any political toes. . . . And of course

I'd gotten to know people on the Hill before I married Tommy and I did a lot of charity stuff. Well, I just got on the list, I guess. Ford Gibson said I was a mascot. He's so sweet. He said no party was complete without me."

"We'd want you to talk about the differences in entertaining by different administrations."

"Oh, *yes*!" Tracy grew even more animated. "What's always so funny is that First Ladies never seem to agree about how the White House should look, although they're always prissy-mouthed about it in public. But they even fight about the place settings. One goes out and one comes in and the one who comes in says, My *God,* her taste was in her *mouth,* and not much of it there, judging by that dinner they invited us to. Would you *look* at the awful china and why did they use that color paint in the family sitting room and we had to redo the entire bathroom for the master bedroom because the damned shower knocks me down when I stand under it and anyway I wanted a pink sunken tub.

"I remember when Linda and Sam moved in, she told me she couldn't *believe* how the Graveses had let the floors go, with all that staff.

"They'd eaten dinner so often on television trays in the family sitting room there were chicken bones under the rugs because they just didn't know how to handle the staff and some of the really good people quit. Then they had the nerve to tell Linda that Helen Graves had left a diamond earring in a drawer in the Queen's bedroom and when they couldn't find it, Linda said you'd have thought it was an FBI case, the fuss they made. And you know, Helen was so forgetful. There was that time she delivered a speech for the Girl Scouts at a senior citizens' convention because she'd forgotten to take last week's speech out of her purse and by the time she got started, it was too late to stop her and George was just *furious.*

"I mean, after all, the Girl Scouts don't exactly form a

voting bloc, do they? After that, they had her press secretary carry her speeches, which meant she had to stay right close to Helen, which wasn't easy. I think she went through five press secretaries. I knew two of them well, and they said it was like dealing with someone who got up every morning and couldn't remember a thing about the previous day. People thought she was a drunk, but she was just dippy. And of course by the time the poor dear got to the White House, she was in her sixties and she'd never been really well. She had this passion for simple American food, as she called it, and I remember one chef quit when she wanted to serve hamburgers at a State dinner."

Tracy stopped for breath and took a small sip of wine. Clayton exchanged meaningful glances with Kennally.

"Tracy," Kennally asked, "did you ever keep a diary?"

She put down her glass, beaming.

"Yes, I did! I was thinking about it the other night in bed when I kept thinking how ridiculous this idea of my writing a book was. I mean, how could I keep track of social history? Then I remembered my diary."

"How long have you been keeping one?" Kennally asked.

"Oh, since I was a teenager. You know, the usual stuff about boyfriends and parties. But after I moved here, I kept it as sort of a record, so I could remember things we'd done and places we'd gone."

"Dates and places?" Kennally asked.

"More than that. It's in code." She laughed a little embarrassedly. "Well, I do think a girl has to protect her privacy, don't you? You never know who's going to start snooping around, and with a teenager in the house, too. I suppose Tommy— Well, I don't know if he looked at it, so I shouldn't accuse him. But anyway, I have a dozen boxes of diaries, I guess."

"What sort of code?"

"My own silly little code. Something nobody but me

could figure out, and sometimes even I have trouble reading it." She giggled.

Clayton suppressed a groan. "You invented the code?" he asked.

She nodded. "It's sort of symbols and initials and words here and there. For example, when I had lunch with you the other day, Clayton, I made a little entry in my diary. I gave it three stars because I enjoyed it so much—sort of like a movie review—and three question marks because you raised such questions in my mind, and the word 'talk' for this book idea and a drawing of a gun for Jared and a tennis racket for Charley Dill, because we'd talked about the Central American business that Charley was going on about the night he got so drunk when there were only three of us left and we had to put him in a taxi. That sort of thing. I could show you."

"I'd like to see them," said Clayton. "But would you be able to translate your code over the years?"

Tracy smiled a little slyly. "I have a very good memory," she said. "I don't act like I do, but I can remember places and dates and who said what to whom almost as well as if I were looking at a photograph. That was probably why I did well in school. I didn't study much, but I could sort of call up notes and pages of textbooks in my head. I suppose it was a little bit like cheating. Anyway, my diaries are sort of a switch in my mind that I can flip on and I remember! Tommy was always astonished how much I could remember when I put my mind to it. He was even more surprised how often I was right!

"I can't always remember little things, like dates or invitations and stuff like that," she admitted. "And I don't have a good sense of direction. Like, I can make a wrong turn on the street I live on. But I remember things nobody expects me to remember."

Clayton looked over at Kennally, whose eyes were fixed on Tracy in fascination.

"I think we should get down to this book as soon as possible, Tracy," he said, raising his eyebrows questioningly at Clayton, who nodded eagerly.

"I think we have the makings of a marvelous social history here. A very important—a very commercial book."

"Really?" Tracy's blue eyes widened and Kennally found himself visualizing her head on a pillow.

"We need an outline," he said. "Clayton will work with you. You just talk and Clayton will get it all on tape and put it into his computer later."

"I can start as soon as Tracy is ready," Clayton said.

Tracy made a graceful little gesture. She had small, butterfly hands, Kennally noticed.

"I can start any time Clayton wants me to. I can always cancel social stuff."

"No," Kennally said quickly. "Don't do that. Go on just as you have. Your social life is part of the book."

"You're really going to *do* this?" Tracy asked tremulously.

Kennally smiled at her. "I think we are. Of course, we need an outline. Then we have to draw up a contract. But with the kind of thing you're been talking about, I think we probably have a deal."

Tracy hesitated, glancing at Clayton, who interpreted for her.

"She— I told her this would be financially lucrative, Jerry," he said.

"I would think so. Does she have an agent?"

Tracy shook her head.

"Well, you understand this is a horseback guess and premature until we get rolling on an outline—" He named a sum in six figures, and Tracy gasped.

"For me?" she gulped.

"Well, for you and Clayton. I assume he'll be your ghostwriter."

"Oh, my *God,* yes. I don't know what I'd do without *Clayton.*"

Clayton smirked.

"We can work out Clayton's share. And of course I shall have to check this with our publisher."

"You work for Robert Mortimer, don't you?" Tracy said. "He's such a nice little man."

Kennally's jaw dropped slightly. "You know him?"

"I've met him. He backed Tim Grotz's campaign in New York. Tim said he couldn't have won without Morty."

"Morty?" Kennally asked.

Tracy laughed. "Oh, I call him that. I told him he looked to me like a Morty and he sort of looked at me in a funny way, then he laughed and we got along fine. He bought me a lovely dinner in New York a couple of times."

Kennally was pleased. He resisted asking *how* well Tracy got along with Mortimer and contended himself with visualizing Mortimer's expression if he were addressed in public as "Morty."

Chapter Seven

The next item about Tracy Gilmartin's forthcoming book was longer than the previous one.

"A lot of VIPs are chewing their nails over which skeletons will come clanking out of whose closets in Tracy Gilmartin's tell-all tome about behind-the-scenes D.C.," read the item in *Spy,* the trendy New York magazine.

"We hear the gorgeous Ms. G. has been privy to all kinds of hanky-panky and is dishing some VERY interesting dirt about movers and shakers on political and diplomatic fronts. All in return for what we hear is a million-dollar advance from put-'em-up tycoon Robert Mortimer, new owner of Grand Old Publishing Company Wissip Golight. The Mighty Mouse, as his critics (yes, he has some) call him, seems to be into the pull-'em-down business these days. There are some who say he should have pulled down some of the things he put up, but you know how people carp. Stay tuned, out there."

The day after the item appeared, Vladimir Mikhail Gostavitch, Soviet ambassador to the United States, sat staring out of the window of his office in the Russian embassy on

Washington's Sixteenth Street. The *Spy* clipping lay on the desk in front of him.

Half a mile away, Samuel Perkins Potter, President of the United States, sat in his office at 1600 Pennsylvania Avenue, staring at the same clipping on his desk in the Oval Office.

On Capitol Hill, United States Senator Eleanor McClusky of Illinois sat with her head in her hands. On her desk lay the same clipping.

All were worried, but only two were uncertain of what to do about the cause of their concern, and she, at that moment, was curled on Clayton Clapper's sofa, enthralling a new audience.

Tracy had never realized how much fun it was to have people listen to her. Clayton wanted to know every detail she could recall, however trivial. Social history was like that, he explained. He laughed uproariously over her story of how the White House had successfully hushed up the impending disaster of the love affair between the youngest daughter of the late President Day Gibbons and a very good-looking young man, who, on the eve of the announcement of their engagement, was found by the FBI to have two wives extant and undivorced in Wyoming and Texas. The biggest problem, recalled Tracy, was preventing the President from horsewhipping his daughter's suitor. When he stopped laughing, Clayton made her go back over her diaries and check her notes and symbols, then tell the whole thing again, slowly. They didn't want any inaccuracies in a social history, he explained. Nothing annoyed readers more. Especially readers who might recognize themselves, he added to himself.

Ambassador Gostavitch wasn't certain he recognized himself in that tantalizing reference to diplomatic movers and shakers, but he couldn't take any chances. He couldn't afford to. He had been guilty of few indiscretions in his life, because they were not only inadvisable, but costly to someone in his position. Unfortunately, Tracy Gilmartin had been one of those indiscretions. He could not risk the possibility that she might disclose or even hint at those occasions when he had succumbed, not only to her charms, but also to his own peculiar personal idiosyncrasy that almost nobody else in the world—certainly not Anna, his wife—knew about.

Gostavitch couldn't believe he had been so stupid, even if he had consumed an enormous amount of Stolichnaya on the night in question. He had known Tracy for years and had lusted after her for a long time. He had yielded to the temptation of the moment and, worst of all, enjoyed it so much that he'd repeated the experience. He could still—with bitterness now—recall Tracy's delectable body, especially when he beheld Anna lumbering across their bedroom in all of her massive nakedness.

He had not seen Tracy for at least a year, but he still thought about her. He remembered her mischievously telling him how she wished she could let him in on a secret that would make him laugh very much indeed, but she never talked about her friends. So much for that. He'd believed her. He'd wanted to believe her. He'd worried, even then, but she had displayed total discretion. Until now. He wondered briefly if he were being premature in his conclusion that she was about to betray him.

Nothing had ever filtered back to him that could have come from Tracy, and he knew too well what a sprinkler system the Washington information pipeline was. But why this item? Why would she be writing a book if she was not prepared to betray friends? The word "diplomatic" had leaped out at him. He felt his skin grow clammy at the thought of the reaction, the ridicule, that would result from Tracy's perfidy. Even in the new liberal climate of *glasnost,* he was likely to be called back to Moscow. Tracy would be considered a potential vehicle of American intelligence. He would be considered a fool and even a traitor. He'd be lucky to wind up in a cubicle deep in the Siberian bureaucracy. His career would be ruined.

It was too high a price to pay for the ephemeral pleasure of illicit sex, preceded by Tracy's merry wielding of a hairbrush. Gostavitch relished and enjoyed his position in Washington. He didn't want to leave. Especially, he didn't want to leave as a laughingstock. He should not have taken the chance in the first place and he would take no more chances. He would not even tolerate the possibility of disclosure, although it seemed alien to the woman he had known and liked so much. She had seemed genuinely sweet and kind, and so loving. . . . He thrust the thought from his mind and picked up the telephone.

He called a member of the embassy staff whose allegiance was to the Russian secret police, a force that had survived the liberalization of attitudes. All that man had to know was that the ambassador had information that this woman had undermined the loyalty of a member of the Soviet delegation with access to top-level security matters, and was in a position to make use of damaging facts. Gostavitch didn't have to say who was involved. All he had to do was make the situation clear. Without Tracy, there could be no book.

In the White House, Senator Giles Macrae of Maine, who had known President Sam Potter since they first came to Congress twenty-six years earlier, was trying to figure out why his old friend was so upset about an item in a gossip column. When Sam called him and asked him to come over as soon as he could, Macrae assumed some political crisis had arisen, not a clipping from what he considered a thoroughly silly rumor mill. But Macrae was a member of that endangered species known as the happily married. He'd never been tempted by women like Tracy Gilmartin.

"So you screwed her," said Macrae. He wished Potter wouldn't chew on the sharp end of a paper knife. "So what? It wasn't last week, was it?"

"Christ, no. Not since I've been in the White House."

"Well, then. I mean, I can see it isn't something you'd want published, but a lot of Presidents have had their peccadilloes and survived, haven't they? It'd only be her word against yours, anyway. Why the fuss? You don't even *know* that's what she's going to write about. This damn thing could be nothing but a teaser for a book that will be mild as milk."

Potter bit down harder on the paper knife, oblivious to Macrae's expression of wrinkled worry. He couldn't tell even Giles, whom he'd trust with just about anything, that what worried him was not an allegation of immorality, but a revelation that the President was partial to kinky sex. He'd always liked to be spanked, preferably with his own clothes brush; he supposed he was accustomed to its bristles. Some women could be odd about that kind of thing, although God knew he had no inclination at all toward sadism and just a tough of masochism. He dated it back to a nurse he'd had as a child.

The only time he'd hinted at this eccentricity to Linda, she'd given him a look of disgust and slept in the guest room. Tracy hadn't been disgusted or angry. She'd been sympathetic and understanding once he'd explained he really didn't want her to hurt him much. She'd given the impression she thought it was funny. As he recalled, the first time had been on the sofa in his old Senate office. He still remembered it with a pleasurable twinge in his rump. In fact, he had nothing but blissful memories of Tracy. Until now. He saw that Macrae was looking at him with a baffled expression.

"I still don't understand the panic."

"Well," Potter said, and stopped.

"She didn't have an abortion, did she?"

Potter shook his head.

"And it was what? Five or six years ago at least?"

Potter nodded.

"Does Linda know?"

Potter shook his head. "Not as far as I know."

"Then *what,* for God's sake?"

Potter looked miserable.

"Maybe I'm making something out of nothing."

Macrae studied him and wondered what Potter wasn't telling him.

"Have you talked to the Gilmartin woman?"

"No."

"Why not? She and Linda are friends, aren't they? Hell, you're all friends now."

"Her line might be bugged."

"So invite her to something. Take her aside. You'll probably find out this is a bunch of nonsense and you've got nothing to worry about. Whatever it is you're really worrying about, Sam."

Potter avoided Macrae's shrewd gray eyes. "I suppose we could do that."

"Well, do it. Invite her to one of this week's social functions."

"The trouble is," the President said bitterly, "she knows everybody. God knows who she's going to nail."

"I keep trying to tell you," Macrae said patiently, "it's a publisher's habit, especially with trash, to put out advance ticklers. Makes people want to buy the book. Makes magazines want to serialize it."

"She did tell Linda it was going to be a party book. Laughed about it, said it was silly."

"Why not take her word for it, then?"

"But this is a campaign year, for God's sake. I know the polls show I'm a shoo-in, but that can change. We've had that problem with the Clapper story on Central America that we're trying to control. And there's that right-wing evangelist Gusty running around the country telling people he's for God and America and God's for him, and the polls show he's moving up. Think what *he* could do with this."

"True," Macrae allowed. "It's a political year and you can't take chances. But let's keep in mind that if you really think you've got possible trouble here—and I don't think you're telling me all of it, Sam—you still might be able to—ah—dissuade the lady."

Potter frowned. "Then she'll say I tried to bribe her."

"No, no, nothing so crude. I understand her husband has taken off for parts unknown and that his departure is permanent."

"So I heard."

"So she's probably hurting for cash. That's probably what's behind this. I mean, I barely know Tracy Gilmartin, but she never struck me as one of the local bitches. Quite the opposite, in fact."

Potter signed deeply. "That's the trouble."

"Well, in that case, as my wife would say, fix her up!"

"What d'you mean?"

"Find her a man. A rich man. Then she won't need to write a book. And she certainly won't want to write anything about those nice people who introduced her to some rich guy, would she?"

"It may be too late," Potter said gloomily. "I suppose we could try. I'll get Linda to put her on a party list. She isn't happy about the book thing either, for that matter."

Macrae looked at him curiously, and bit back the question on his lips.

Potter was tired. He didn't need this kind of crap in the middle of an election year that he had thought wouldn't pose any problem at all. And Linda was being more difficult than usual. When they sat down to dinner in the family quarters of the White House that night, she seemed on edge, complaining about her schedule, even about the filet of sole on her plate.

"What's the matter?" he asked.

"Nothing." She spat the word out.

He chewed moodily on a roll. "You see this latest item about Tracy Gilmartin's book?"

He saw a mixture of anger and anxiety in Linda's eyes and wondered what Tracy knew about his wife.

"Yes. Why?"

"Just curious. I recall you seemed upset about the last one."

"Why would *I* be upset?"

"You did point out she knew a lot of people, as I recall. That was why you asked her about it."

Linda put down her fork and picked up her wineglass.

"Yes, I did. And what she said didn't sound remotely like what that damned column said yesterday."

"Maybe they're just trying to drum up readership."

"I expect they are."

"I was thinking," said Potter, "Maybe we ought to put Tracy on the list for the State dinner for the President of Iceland this week."

Linda's brown eyes narrowed. "Why?"

"Maybe she needs to be reminded who her friends are. Maybe she might sit next to somebody who'd take her mind off Tommy."

Linda looked at him with respect.

"Maybe you're right! I expect she is lonely. Maybe she's worried about money. I don't know that they ever had that much and Tommy lived pretty well. Now that he's gone . . ." She looked off into the distance.

"Let me think who'd be right for her."

"Rich."

They smiled at each other with unusual empathy.

The clipping on Eleanor McClusky's desk had been crumpled up and smoothed out so often, the print was faded. She reread it for the twentieth time and told herself again that Tracy, dear Tracy, would never do something like that to her. Eleanor's eye registered with horror that the desk calendar marked this day for her dinner with Uncle Francis Sikorski. She dug in a desk drawer for aspirin, popped two tablets in her mouth, and reached for the telephone to postpone the dinner at the same moment that the door opened and her scheduling secretary entered, propelled by the bulk of the man behind her.

"Senator—it's your—"

Eleanor stood up with a sense of fatality and forced herself to smile.

"Uncle Francis. What a surprise!"

She was enveloped in an embrace redolent of a particularly pungent after-shave lotion.

"Ellie! We got in early and your aunt is having her hair done. I thought I'd just pop over to your office since I've never had a good look at it, maybe get a little personal tour of the Senate from one of its most distinguished members!"

Eleanor recoiled from the gleaming smile and the cobra eyes, noting Sikorski had dressed in what he considered suitable apparel. He wore a black Italian silk suit and a pale gray silk tie.

"Met a nice young guy outside your office. Said he was from the *Chicago Tribune.* He was waiting to interview you. Real interested to hear I was your uncle."

"He'd heard of you, of course," said Eleanor. Uncle Francis's grin broadened until she wondered how many teeth he actually had in his head. They seemed far in excess of the usual number.

"He surely had. Sikorski dry-cleaning outlets are all over our state, Ellie, as you know."

And dry cleaning wasn't their primary purpose—she knew that, too. She was certain the *Chicago Tribute* would be fascinated by the knowledge that Sikorski was visiting Washington in the role of a senator's uncle. Her only comfort was that she knew she'd be asked about Sikorski's presence. She edged away from Sikorski, who followed her as though afraid she'd flee out the door.

"I have to do that interview, Uncle Francis, so if you could excuse me for a little while—maybe you could take a stroll around the Hill—it's a nice day . . ." she heard herself babbling.

Sikorski nodded benignly. "I told the young fellow how proud we all were of you."

He wandered about the office, looking at photographs on the walls, studying a portrait of Eleanor with the President.

"Got to have an autographed copy of that for *my* office!"

It would be a cold day in hell when he did, she thought, as she smiled at him. He stared unashamedly at the papers on her desk that she had begun hastily shuffling together. The clipping about Tracy floated to the floor. He picked it up and read it before she could seize it.

"What's this about?"

"Oh, nothing. Just nonsense." She tried to retrieve the clipping, as Sikorski's black eyes roved over it and flicked up to her face.

"Who's this Tracy Gilmartin broad?"

"She—she's sort of a society woman here."

"You going to be in this book she's writing?"

"Heavens, no! Why would she be writing about me?" Eleanor's voice was calm, but her hands were damp.

"She a friend of yours?"

"I thought she was." The words popped out in involuntary bitterness, and were not lost on Sikorski. He jabbed a thick finger at the battered clipping.

"You clipped this. Why? I mean, it's none of my business, but you seem sorta upset about it."

"Of course not, Uncle Francis! It's just that gossip books can be a nuisance politically. Whether they're accurate or not, they misrepresent people and facts, and, well, I'm sure you know how when the public gets hold of any gossip, they view it as fact. We all have to keep an eye open for that kind of thing on the Hill, that's all."

She prayed she sounded as though she was offering a

casual explanation. It said something about how much that clipping had gotten to her that she was talking about it at all with Sikorski. She hadn't seen Tracy in a while. She'd meant to call her, sympathize with her about Tommy's leaving, but Charley Dill's report of how Tracy had reassured Linda Potter hadn't entirely eased Eleanor's mind. She was uncertain about getting in touch with Tracy, although she thought she ought to. The memory of that night remained with her. What had it meant to Tracy? Suppose the next item mentioned a lesbian in the Senate?

Eleanor knew that wasn't a hanging offense nowadays. There were self-proclaimed gay men in both houses of Congress. But if there was another woman in Congress who preferred women, she didn't know about it. And it wasn't as if she were out cruising the bars. She was the soul of discretion. She dated men, although she didn't go to bed with them. She knew only that she couldn't bear it, for many reasons, if Tracy talked. She lifted her eyes to the probing black gaze of Uncle Francis Sikorski.

"You upset about somethin', Ellie?" he asked solicitously.

She shook her head, mustered another smile. Her mouth felt tight.

"I'm just harried today. Lot going on. You know how it is."

"You worried about this thing?" Sikorski, a man not easily distracted from what he had decided was the point at issue, gestured toward the clipping.

"Of course not! How ridiculous!"

"You'd rather she didn't write this book, right?"

"I don't care one way or the other. I don't know why we're even discussing it. It's none of my business what she does. It's just, as I told you, that in politics you have to be so careful. Things can be twisted so you lose the truth, and I have no idea what Tracy's up to. I should really call and have a drink with her and chat about it all. Probably all nonsense in the column." She was babbling again. "Now let's talk about more important things. We have to settle on a place for dinner—"

Uncle Francis beamed at her. "All taken care of. I had my secretary do it from Chicago yesterday. In your name, although of course we're taking you. But I've heard about that Maison Blanche place and I wanted to go somewhere you'd be comfortable."

Eleanor gulped.

"How . . . very thoughtful of you," she said.

Uncle Francis kissed her on the cheek before she could move aside, and she sneezed at the wave of after-shave.

"You haven't got a cold, have you?"

She shook her head, fumbling for a Kleenex and pressing it over her nose like a gas mask.

"Then we'll see you at eight, okay? Your aunt's all excited! And Ellie?"

Ellie looked at him wearily as he smiled his deadly smile.

"Don't you worry yourself about that Gilmartin book, okay?"

She nodded. "I won't, Uncle Francis."

Still smiling, he left, and she shuddered as she heard him bestowing a warm greeting on the reporter from the *Chicago Tribune*. It was not until a few moments later, when she was trying to compose her mind and her face, that she realized the clipping was missing.

Chapter Eight

She had always loved White House parties, especially State dinners, which could be a heady blend of formality and fun. The invitation had come as a surprise, only three days before the event, and it was accompanied by a note from Linda Potter explaining there had been a mix-up in the list and she so hoped Tracy would be free because she was looking forward to seeing her. Tracy was delighted. She was even more pleased when a White House car arrived to pick her up. She assumed that was the First Lady's playful way of reminding her of the time she had forgotten the date of another invitation.

Tracy's smile lit up the limousine as it rolled up the White House driveway and deposited her in the courteous hands of white-uniformed aides who escorted her to the receiving line presided over by the President and First Lady. Tracy felt pampered and cosseted and loved. This was her world, and these were her friends, or at least some of them were. She accepted a glass of champagne from a silver tray carried by a black-coated butler and waved gaily at familiar faces. She admired the elaborate floral arrangements on which Linda Potter prided herself, and happily let herself be absorbed into the decorously moving crowd. She observed the usual judicious mix of celebrities, politicians, contributors, and social pretenders, the men interchangeable as zippers in black tie, the women cast in the social and psychological role of butterflies.

Linda Potter, regal in hyacinth blue satin that bared one tanned shoulder, flung her arms around Tracy, proclaiming her joy at seeing her and her glee at having made her the only guest to receive personal transportation to the White House.

They chortled and chirruped together before Tracy was expertly propelled onward to the President, who kissed her cheek and complimented her on her dress, a flame-colored silk which complemented the warm earth tones of table linens and gold candles in the State dining room.

Tracy drifted into the crowd and noticed that several people asked her about her book, which pleased her because it meant they were taking her writing seriously. That, according to her mentor, Clayton, was important to a social historian. She assured them she was working hard, and they smiled. Willie Temple, escorting a young actress whose spiky pink hair matched a pink dress with very little back and not much front, laughed and patted Tracy's cheek possessively.

"Little Tracy writing a book!" he said. Tracy's smile almost faded.

Political columnist Dick Gilt, there with his television-anchor wife, Pauline Litvak, as the rotating White House concession to the fourth estate at such dinners, came bustling over with unusual urgency.

"Tracy, what's this we're hearing about a book? I thought you were the soul of discretion?" he demanded.

"That's a gorgeous dress," said his wife, a tawny blond woman whose success in her career was attributed to her magnificent self-possession on camera.

Tracy maintained her smile.

"It isn't a question of discretion at all. It's not a book about gossip. It's a—social history," she replied, and hoped she didn't sound as defensive as she was beginning to feel.

Gilt laughed, "You're joking!" he said. "What d'you mean, a social history? *You're* writing a social history, Tracy? Washington's best party girl? Give me a break!"

Tracy had never been fond of Dick Gilt since she'd decided he was unkind to Jeanne. She was beginning to dislike him intensely, which was uncharacteristic. Tracy rarely felt hostility toward people. She was fond of saying there was something to like in everyone, a remark that had exasperated her husband. But in those days nobody had challenged her intelligence. They'd simply assumed she didn't have much.

"My publishers seem to think I'm qualified to write social history, Dick," she said frigidly. She surprised herself by adding, "You don't have to be a columnist to have opinions, you know."

Gilt looked taken aback, and Tracy seized the opportunity to move to another group, which, she discovered too late, included not only Linda Potter but Jayne Millspaw. Tracy felt uneasy around Jayne, who greeted her with the smile of a hospitable tiger.

"Tracy, *darling*," Jayne gushed. "You are just the talk of the town."

"Mmmm," said Linda, "we were just talking about you. We're all dying to hear more about your book, dear."

Tracy looked at their smoothly smiling faces and swallowed hard.

"I keep trying to tell everybody it really *is* a social history. Party recollections. Just fun."

"Sounds hilarious," said the First Lady. "And are your writing this all by yourself, dear?"

"Oh, no. I have Clayton. He does the writing. I just talk," Senator Charley Dill materialized at her elbow. "Clayton Clapper?" he asked

"He's wonderful," Tracy said enthusiastically. "It was really all his idea."

"I'm sure it was," said the senator.

"He's very conscientious," Tracy assured him. She wanted to make clear this was a book where facts were checked out. She was getting tired of being considered frivolous.

"But Tracy," said Linda, "I still don't understand what this book is going to be about. I mean, are you writing about people, or parties, or what?"

"All kinds of things," Tracy explained earnestly. "What Clayton calls my perceptions of people I've known over the years. Anecdotes as illustrations of political moods, as Jerry calls them."

"Jerry?" asked Linda.

"Jerry Kennally. My editor at Wissip Golight. You know, they call it WG. A very old firm." Tracy's voice held a trace of pride.

"That's the one that Mortimer took over," Jayne noted, sipping champagne with her bright black eyes fixed on Tracy's face.

"And I remember Jerry Kennally," she went on. "Tall, good-looking Englishman. Fleet Street type. Breezed through Washington before he and Mortimer discovered each other."

"That's right," Tracy agreed. "Isn't he charming?"

"Very," said Jayne, and smiled.

"Fleet Street," Charley Dill said dejectedly, adjusting the bow of his black tie. He reflected that pinning Tracy down was like capturing a blob of mercury. You weren't sure whether she was very smart or very stupid, and unfortunately, given lack of evidence of the former, everybody had assumed the latter. The linking of Tracy to Clayton Clapper reminded him of Eleanor McClusky's uneasiness and sounded a warning bell in his mind. He still could not imagine Tracy tapping out more than a chronicle of trivia, but Clapper had the journalistic experience and sharpness to mine information from mush.

Tracy's book was beginning to take on a different dimension in Dill's mind, and he was reassessing his dismissal of her as a leak. She could be that most potentially dangerous property of all—a source unaware of what she knew, scattering conversational snackies that would be snapped up by anyone who recognized their worth and content.

Charley made a mental note to avoid Tracy in the future when he was in his cups. He tried unsuccessfully to recall whether she had been around when he sounded off on the subject of Sam Potter's idiocy about Central America to what he had assumed was a small group of close friends drinking brandy after a dinner party in Georgetown. The thing was that Tracy was around so much, you hardly noticed her. She was, as somebody had said, like the centerpiece on the table. But what if the centerpiece were bugged? Charley sighed. A talking Tracy could do serious political damage to a lot of people. Clapper's reputation as a reporter was based on his capacity for furious digging, which made his partnership with Tracy ominous.

Linda Potter had given her personal attention to the seating chart for the dinner for the President of Iceland, making sure Tracy was seated next to Dimitri Stavropoulos, whom she and Jayne Millspaw had chosen as their candidate to take a woman's mind off literary pursuits. Stavropoulis, known as Dim, was a tall Greek who looked a good deal like Anthony Quinn and didn't hesitate to make the most of the resemblance. He was, observed Jayne, the Greekest Greek she'd ever met.

"There is no occasion at which he won't get up and do that damned dance," she said acidly.

Dim's fondness for bright and beautiful women was legendary. He had amassed a collection of them over the years that aroused awe as well as envy. Dim loved celebrities. He liked to have on his arm a woman who was not only glamorous, but also well known. The more controversial, the better. He was uninterested in the kind of women he dismissed as bedtime bimbos. He liked his women to be able to talk; he would not exchange an evening of conversational boredom for the prospect of pleasure between the sheets.

Dim sought the unusual and the unattainable, which he considered a challenge. A brilliant woman who was married to someone else was catnip to Dim. He had pulled off a personal coup by persuading the wife of a multimillionaire banker to leave her husband for him. Marcia was a sophisticated, lovely woman whose physical attributes were transcended only by the sharpness of her mind and her cold-bloodedness. To Dim's outrage, she tired of him first. She was distasteful of his flamboyance, his lack of inhibition, his exuberantly intemperate passions, and what she called his money grubbing.

That had really stung, because Dim was justifiably proud of the financial acumen that had involved him in dexterously diversified investments, during the days before oil prices plummeted, and doubled his already massive wealth. Money was so boring, said Marcia, who had always been surrounded by piles of it. One morning she left and sought a reconciliation with her banker husband. His self-esteem was so inflated by her discarding of the legendary Dim for his unobtrusive self that he welcomed her home and noted with quiet amusement that she brought with her a million-dollar souvenir of *l'affaire Dim* in the form of diamonds showered on her by the besotted Greek. She declined to return them, explaining that she considered them symbols of their continuing mutual affection.

Consequently, Dim was less ebullient, less supremely confident of himself, than usual. His experience with the remotely beautiful Marcia had not exactly discouraged him, but he had been married three times and indulged in countless liaisons, and he was beginning to chafe at the cost of feminine companionship. His wives appeared to consider the marriage contract a license to steal, and he was too proud to propose a prenuptial agreement. There were limits even to the generosity of a Stavropoulos, and he was smarting, an unfamiliar sensation to one accustomed to cresting life on a wave of personal, professional, and sexual success. He looked with somber dark eyes at his friend Linda Potter when she told him she wanted him to meet a friend of hers.

"Women are not my friends," he said gloomily. "Did I tell you that Marcia—"

"Yes, yes, you did, Dim, and I am just appalled," Linda said quickly before he embarked on yet another catalog of the wrongs done to him. "But *this* woman is different."

"Hah," said Dim.

"Believe me," said Linda, "She is like you in a way. She has been betrayed by her husband. Abandoned. For a *man*."

"A man!" Dim spat.

Linda glanced at the rug and sighed. "She is an old friend of mine. She is perfectly beautiful, and very sweet, and everyone loves her. We are upset about her, just as we're upset about you, Dim, darling. So we thought you might—you know?—comfort each other. that's all."

"No marriage," Dim said flatly.

"Of course not," said Linda. "She isn't even divorced, anyway. She's just lonely and hurt and unhappy. She needs someone like you. A strong man like you."

"Beautiful. But can she talk? Some women have nothing to say that cannot be said in two minutes. Even in bed, one should be able to talk."

"Tracy can talk, and she's certainly not boring. Why, she's writing a book right now about her experiences in Washington. I understand she got a big advance on it from a New York publisher too."

"She is a gossip columnist?" Dim brightened. He loved

celebrity gossip, considering it the spice of serious conversation.

"No, she isn't. But she knows everybody. She says she's writing a social history of Washington. Whatever that is," Linda added under her breath.

"Ah," Dim's interest seemed to be rising. "A social historian, eh? An observer of the American scene? And beautiful too?"

"Very," said Linda. "Trust me."

Dim decided his trust had not been misplaced when he found his dinner partner was a small, voluptuous, yet slender woman with a halo of blond hair, peach-smooth skin, of which a good deal could be seen when she leaned forward, and immense blue eyes that she fastened attentively on his face the minute he opened his mouth.

"How do you do?" Dim was always formal. "I am Dimitri Stavropoulos."

She gave him her hand, which was small and slim and silken, and her smile, which was wide and warm and bright. "And I'm Tracy Gilmartin. I'm happy to meet you."

Their romance took root over the smoked salmon mousse, budded with the truffled capon, and bloomed over the chocolate decadence, nurtured by a sprinkling of excellent wines. Tracy thought Dim was the most fascinating, sexy man she had met in years, and Dim thought Tracy was one of the most delicious, responsive women he had ever encountered, especially by comparison with his recent alliance with the Snow Queen, Marcia. There was nothing he said that didn't seem to interest Tracy, and her responses were appropriate. She was surprisingly well informed, partly because she made it a habit to read the front page of the newspaper as well as the feature columns, and she had always absorbed more of what she heard than she realized, as Clayton Clapper had discovered.

A recent dinner-table conversation with a high-level official in the Federal Reserve had, for example, provided her with enough background information to be aware of Dim's skill in avoiding the financial disaster that had overtaken some of his fellow financiers.

As the guests moved from dining to dancing beneath the crystal chandeliers of the East Room, President Potter and his wife watched Dim's dark head bending close to Tracy's. Dim did not allow her to leave his side until Potter strolled over and announced he was going to exercise his presidential prerogative and refuse to allow one of the most beautiful women there to be so monopolized. Dim was not displeased, as Potter had intended. And as Tracy moved lightly in his arms, the President looked into her luminous eyes with less remembered pleasure than usual and asked how her book was coming along.

"Slowly, slowly," responded Tracy. "Clayton says I don't stay on the point long enough, and he has to keep retracing stuff with me. He's very careful, of course, and I tend to chatter on. But that's apparently what they want."

"I was a little puzzled," the President said casually, "by that item in *Spy* the other day. Made it sound as if you were playing kiss and tell on all your old friends, my dear."

Tracy was genuinely disconcerted. "Why, Sa—Mr. President, how can you say something like that?" she protested, "That was the silliest column I ever saw. You know what *Spy*'s like. They don't get the facts, they just get your attention."

Potter wondered whether that observation was original with Tracy. She went on to confirm his suspicion.

"Anyway, that's what Clayton and Jerry say. And if it weren't for them, I'd never have thought of writing *anything*. I'd never have thought I had anything worth saying if it weren't for them."

"Who's Jerry?"

"He's my editor. He used to be a very well known journalist in London."

"He's the one who says you're a social historian."

She nodded.

"I hope you aren't letting those people take advantage of you, Tracy."

She looked puzzled, and a little resentful. "Why is everybody making such a fuss about my writing my own observations? I mean, other people have written their memoirs and nobody paid attention. It's just a question of a different viewpoint. Things I remember that people have forgotten."

The problem was, Potter thought, she remembered things people would just as soon have forgotten.

"But you can be dealing with what are still private conversations. Things that should stay private."

"What about that editor who wrote about private conversations he had with a President?"

"The President was dead, at least."

Her face softened suddenly, and a smile curved her mouth. "Oh, Sam," she whispered, so that only he could hear her. "Don't be ridiculous. *I* know what you mean. I'd never write about anything like that!"

Despite the softness of her voice, Potter glanced uneasily about. He applied his mouth to the blond curl concealing her ear. "It's not what *you*'d write," he murmured. "It's what Clayton would write."

Tracy drew back with a look of reproof. "Clayton wouldn't write anything I didn't want him to."

But Clayton apparently already had talked her into believing she was a social historian, the President reflected. He had the discretion not to say so.

"Just keep in mind it's still you who's saying what will be in this book, Tracy. I mean, these people want to make money by publishing this kind of stuff—this history, I mean. I'm sure *you* would never try to cause trouble, but I want to make sure you know what you're doing—that you aren't being used."

Tracy's lower lip jutted slightly. "I'm really not as stupid as some people seem to think I am, Mr. President," she said. As the music stopped, she made a little half-bow and turned and glided across the polished parquet into the eager arms of Dim Stavropoulos.

Potter turned to find his wife at his elbow, wearing her social smile.

"What's she say?" she asked.

"She said she's writing a social history. Guided by a former Fleet Street reporter and ghostwritten by one of our more aggressive investigative Washington journalists."

"Oh, Christ," said Linda.

"That's my feeling too. I don't honestly think there's any malice in *her*. I think she's been brainwashed into seeing herself as a social commentator."

"So she's just saying anything she can remember to Clapper and he's taping it."

"That's what it sounds like. I don't know whether he's written anything or whether they're still at the taping stage. She seems genuinely surprised to be asked about it. Let's just hope Dim works out."

They looked toward Tracy and Dim, who were intertwined as closely as a public setting would permit.

"I have faith in Dim," said Linda. She had been wondering for some time whether her dalliance with a certain diplomat, as well as the pilot of Air Force One, might be included in the confidences that Tracy the social historian was bestowing on Clayton Clapper. Linda remembered exchanging intimate observations with Tracy about pilot John Moore, who had left few females untouched in the swath he cut through Washington's social boredom. It didn't matter if Tracy admitted she'd been one of John's small army of conquests, but it would matter if she mentioned with that happy giggle that he'd done the same thing to the First Lady.

The frustrating thing about Tracy talking was that nobody, including Tracy herself, most likely, had any idea of what she'd say or whether she realized what she'd said.

The bottom line was that her ghostwriter and her editor could be relied on to know what Tracy had told them.

Linda looked over her husband's shoulder to where Dim was swaying almost imperceptibly with Tracy. She gave him a tiny wave and a wink and was encouraged when his swarthy face split into a grin of pure delight.

Dim was happy. Tracy was amusing, affectionate as a kitten, interesting to talk to, and lovely to look at. He could hardly wait to take her home. On an inspiration, he suggested they drive to Annapolis so that she could see his yacht by moonlight. Tracy loved yachts, and Dim's was one of the larger and more luxurious. They even looked briefly at the moon before retiring below so that Dim could discover Tracy was as lovely to look at without clothes.

For her part, Tracy was swept away by the kind of ardor she had never encountered before. Dim behaved as if he had personally invented her, and he took pride in his creation. They drank champagne when they weren't making love and spent most of the next day in bed. Tracy was drunk with happiness, and Dim was entranced by the difference between her and his most recent lover. He had to keep reminding himself, delightedly, that it was lovable Tracy and not mean Marcia who was snuggling in his arms.

In the days that followed, nothing was farther from Tracy's mind than her contribution to the social history of the nation's capital. She probably wouldn't have noticed if Washington had been engulfed by an earthquake. Their only excursion from the yacht was when Dim took a shopping trip for clothes she'd never been able to afford before, so he could enjoy removing them as soon as she put them on. Her world was circumscribed by Dim's embraces and she didn't even check her answering service, or she would have been aware of several anguished messages.

"I'm going to call the police and report her missing," Clayton told Jerry Kennally, who laughed.

"Don't be silly," Kennally said comfortably. "She'll come home, wagging her little tail behind her."

"But she hasn't even called me! We had appointments—"

"Clayton," Kennally said soothingly, "she's screwing this Greek. Leave the woman alone, let her enjoy herself. She couldn't have had much fun with what's his name, who's having it off with some pianist in British Columbia, for God's sake."

"She hasn't exactly been living in a nunnery," said Clayton sulkily. He'd been trying to transcribe tapes and having trouble. Tracy's concept of recollection was convoluted, and he was worried. Without her, he could not comfortably put facts into the computer. "How could she do this to me?" he complained. "I'm on leave from the paper, I'm unable to do anything, and she doesn't even have the decency to stay in touch with me."

"She will, she will," said Kennally. "One of them'll get bored."

"Why are you so sure of that?"

"She's just off on a toot," said Kennally. "Go have a drink and stop worrying. You're brooding like an old hen."

Clayton looked guiltily at the knitting he resorted to in moments of stress. Kennally was probably right, but Clayton remained worried about Tracy, who had become his source of financial support. The outline had produced a respectable advance, but a significant sum would follow only after the arrival of part of the manuscript, and while Clayton was still confident Tracy would pay off in the long run, in the short haul, she was making a nervous wreck of him.

In the White House there was quiet joy over Tracy's disappearance. With every succeeding day, the Potters' spirits rose.

"I told you," said Linda.

"You think he might take her to that island he has in the Aegean?" the President said hopefully.

"Made for each other," said his wife, who had been having congratulatory lunches with Jayne Millspaw for a week. Even Jayne conceded the plan seemed to have been successful, yet being Jayne, she remained skeptical.

"Let's hope they're screwing," she said.

"What else would they be doing?" the First Lady asked.

Jayne considered the possibilities.

"Well," she said, "you know Dim does love gossip. Let's hope she isn't talking to *him*."

Chapter Nine

Fourteen days after she met Dimitri Stavropoulos, Tracy went home to a pile of unpaid bills, an unfilial letter from her daughter, a postcard of British Columbia from her husband, and four bulbs that had burned out after she'd left the lights on in her excitement as she flitted out in her flame-colored gown to purr away in a White House limousine. Her romance with Dim had not turned out quite the way she expected. God knew she never imagined she would want to get away from someone who liked to listen to her talk. But increasingly that was what Dim wanted to do. It was *all* he wanted to do, and it made her uneasy. It was flattering when Clayton and Jerry encouraged her to talk, because that was for her book. But it was crushing to her bruised ego when her new lover preferred to lie back on his silk pillows and laugh over her anecdotes about past parties instead of making the kind of impassioned love to her that left her dizzy but happy.

It amused her at first when Dim was curious about her social history book and she relished his rumbles of mirth as she related stories of hushed-up social catastrophes, such as those that had taken place at a dignified party for a foreign visitor, given by a Washington grande dame. A new chef's weakness for smoking pot led to his experimenting with an unpredictable chemical substance that he sprinkled lightheartedly into the champagne. The guest of honor was the first to sink into a condition in which he sang a bawdy song, then crawled under the table. The hostess herself had danced a tango on her dining room table before collapsing amidst the Waterford crystal.

The only comfort to be drawn from the fiasco, Tracy recalled, was that the presence of the managing editors of both Washington newspapers proved of incalculable value in preventing the public disclosure of the events of the evening. The guilty chef, found humming happily in the kitchen, was transferred to his employer's country estate for enrollment in a drug program so that he wouldn't spread the news.

Dim laughed until he cried, especially when she identified some of the guests, including a columnist as pompous as he was prominent, who reacted to the drugged champagne by drawing mustaches with his gold fountain pen on a substantial number of his hostess's art treasures.

Over the next week, Tracy had begun to feel like Scherazade, who had to tell a story a day in order to keep her head. The morning she woke up hoarse and saw Dim smiling in his sleep beside her, Tracy began to feel used. She suspected that Dim had known so many women, their bodies rapidly lost urgent interest for him and he welcomed variations on the sexual theme. That probably accounted for his passion for Marcia, whom he had told Tracy about, and who read the financial pages in bed, with Dim's approval. Tracy's variation apparently was that she could tell stories. Not about herself—his interest in her own background was minimal—but about other people, famous people, many of whom Dim knew. But he didn't know as much about them as she did, and he couldn't wait to find out.

He still stroked her body, but his mind was on what she could tell him. She remembered Sam Potter's warning about being used, although he had not intended it to be applied to Dim. She decided that what she represented was an encyclopaedic memory with curves. At least Clayton wanted her to talk for research and mutual profit, and she enjoyed that because it made her feel that if what she knew mattered, she mattered.

To Dim, she was a serial gossip column. She decided it was time for her to go home. She was honest enough to admit she was not in love with Dim. He had initially done wonders for her self-esteem, then demolished her burgeoning self-confidence because his passion for her stories exceeded his passion for her. Yet she enjoyed most of the time she spent with him, which certainly had been a revelation in terms of sexual enjoyment, and she left with a certain regret.

While he was still sleeping, she borrowed his limousine and driver, returned to Washington, and sent a polite note back in the car thanking him for his hospitality. She left on the yacht, a little sadly, the clothes he had bought her because she felt, with memories of her mother stirring in her mind, that it would not be quite proper to take them with her. She retained the hope he might send them on to her, since he had little use for them unless he knew someone else of the same size, which of course was a possibility. He probably had closets full of clothes for female friends. But she liked Dim, and Tracy was not given to holding grudges. She replaced the burned-out light bulbs, threw away the bills, took a hot shower, and telephoned Clayton.

His joyful reaction to the sound of her voice almost made up for her disappointment in Dim.

"Tracy!" he called "I've been so worried! Where are you?"

"I'm home. I'm back," she said sedately.

"My God, I can't tell you how delighted I am. Jerry and I have been frantic," he assured her with partial truth.

"I got—sort of tied up. Well, I expect you heard. It's probably all over town." She had no illusions about Clayton's ability to find out precisely where she had gone and with whom.

"Well, I sort of heard. I mean, I really was worried when you didn't show up that morning, so I made a few inquiries. I wanted to be sure you were all right."

Tracy sighed. "Clayton, I'm glad you took the trouble to find out because probably nobody else would've bothered."

"Did you—ah—have a good time?" He couldn't resist asking.

She giggled that familiar rippling giggle of hers. "Most of it. God, Clayton, this'll kill you, but you know what I finally couldn't stand? He wanted me to tell him about my book! He was more interested in my—my social history than me!"

"He's a fool," said Clayton gallantly. "How much did you tell him?"

"Oh, just ancient gossip that I thought everybody knew. You know, like the disaster the night the chef put dazzle dust in the champagne and everybody went wild at Gale's dinner."

Clayton relaxed a little. "You know, Tracy," he said earnestly, "we have to be careful. You know the gossip columns have been leaking stuff—"

"Didn't Jerry give it to them?" she asked bluntly.

"Well—Jerry would be careful. I mean, he considers this a—a serious book. The trouble is that they get a fact and just twist it around. Believe me, I know how it's done."

Tracy grinned at his candor. "I don't think I told Dim anything that's going to detract from what we're doing," she assured him.

"And now we *are* going to get back to work?" Clayton's voice was anxious. Tracy felt guilty. She had let Clayton down, after all he had done for her. If it hadn't been for

Clayton, she wouldn't have prospects of money coming in at all. There hadn't been a penny from Tommy, despite his promises, and she'd been off cavorting with a gossip-mad Greek millionaire.

"Let me get a couple of things straightened out in the house and I'll be over first thing in the morning. Breakfast."

"I'll make pancakes," Clayton offered.

Tracy thought of Dim's cook and sighed. "Wonderful," she said, and unplugged the telephone before she went to bed that night. She doubted Dim would pursue her. She was sure that for Dim there was always a substitute. But she hadn't had much sleep for a couple of weeks, between sex and storytelling, and she'd always figured when she didn't have a good reason for being awake, she might as well be getting her sleep.

She arrived at Clayton's house full of apologies and good intentions and found him reading a *New York Times* analysis of the presidential ambitions of Winston Gusty, a charismatic conservative televangelist who appeared to constitute a challenge to Sam Potter in the forthcoming campaign.

"Does he have a real chance?" asked Tracy as Clayton leapt up to hug her and usher her to a table that seemed laden with pancakes.

"He might. The polls show he's doing far better than anybody expected, especially the pundits who said Americans would never vote for one of the religious nuts. He covers it up a lot better, and he's got more political horse sense. I mean, he's for family and God and clean living and all that, but he's never gone the route of stopping the whirlwind and talking to the Almighty and that kind of bullshit. He's a religious pragmatic and that's a formidable combination. I guess you could say he keeps an eye on the polls while he prays. Reagan won with less to work with."

Tracy poured syrup over a pancake. "Mmmm. You're a great cook, Clayton." She chewed thoughtfully for a moment. "Gus is a pragmatist, you're right about that. He thinks before he talks," she said.

Clayton looked up. "Gus?"

"I always called him Gus. I got to know him when he was campaigning last year and I was visiting my mother. She thought he was just wonderful—of course, he eased her conscience because she's a fallen-away Mormon—but she's also pretty shrewd. She was stuffing envelopes for the Gusty people."

"How well did you know him?"

Clayton looked at her with hope and wonder. Sometimes he thought of Tracy as his own private miracle. She laughed, and he surreptitiously turned on his tape recorder.

"Well, I didn't take him too seriously, I mean, my God, how do you take politicians seriously? That sort of annoyed him at first, because of course he takes himself seriously. Then he realized I wasn't trying to be critical or unkind, and that I was rather curious about him—"

"And he wound up telling you his life story?" Clayton interrupted with a grin.

Tracy's blue eyes sparkled. "My, yes. And once he realized he didn't have to pretend he was the son of God, he was very interesting. You're right when you say he has one eye on the polls when he prays. He told me once that he realized God and politics would make great bedfellows. So to speak."

Clayton chuckled. "He really is the saintly family man? No skeletons?"

Tracy giggled. "Not really. Sort of the lust in his heart stuff more than anything else. But he has his little weaknesses."

"Such as?"

"Southern Comfort, for one thing."

"What about all that stuff about bringing back the era of teetotalism as a means of crushing the drug dangers?"

"Yes, well, of course, he'd say that because it goes down well with the Bible Belt, or that's what he told me. But let me tell you, he and I once did a little drinking together, and you know I don't drink much. Or very well!"

"You drank Southern Comfort with Gusty?" He stared at her.

"I told him I'd never tasted it. It was the end of a long day. I'd been helping out because my mother was sick and we wound up in his office with the door locked and Southern Comfort on the desk. It was really funny. We both got looped."

"And?" Clayton's eyes were glittering.

"Well, he chased me around the desk a couple of times and then he caught me! God, he was funny!" Tracy put down her fork. "Clayton," she said, "I like Gus. You can't put this in the book!"

Clayton shrugged. "I've heard it around town, that he's susceptible to a little comfort of one kind or another," he said untruthfully. What he knew he had was a story that had never come out about Winston Gusty, boy wonder of the television church, who preached religion and expounded politics on a podium where the backdrop gave the impression he had golden wings. The press thought it was uproarious. The faithful thought it was prophetic.

"Oh, really?" Tracy raised her eyebrows. "Well, I suppose I wasn't the only one. Not that I thought I was. But I did have the impression that he was a pretty straight arrow. I thought maybe I was an aberration."

"In the office?" Clayton asked.

Tracy's eyes twinkled. "On the desk."

They both erupted into laughter.

"Well"— Tracy was philosophical— "all politicians have their weaknesses, as I said. I guess it must be hard to live up to the kind of image they try to build of themselves. I mean, who's morally photogenic?"

Clayton nodded. He'd noticed that Tracy was becoming

more interesting to listen to, as she translated her experiences into opinions. He looked at her with genuine affection; his little golden goose. They spent a busy day, with Tracy painstakingly combing her diaries and her memory to compensate for her recent abandonment of Clayton.

He was able to report to Jerry Kennally that night that everything was back on track and moving smoothly.

"Mortimer's anxious to see something on paper soon. He's a bottom-line man. The only sentences he reads with interest are punctuated by dollar signs," said Kennally.

"Today was great," Clayton told him. "I should be able to get a decent sample to you by next week. But we've got to be careful with her."

"Mortimer can stand a lawsuit," said Kennally. "All the more publicity. Might get him on the talk shows. That's his real ambition."

Clayton told him about Tracy and Winston Gusty and the Southern Comfort, and Kennally hooted.

"Oh, my God, that's wonderful!" He took a note or two, and a few days later, the equivalent of fire and brimstone erupted at the Gusty campaign headquarters when the candidate read an item in *Spy* that elevated him to the ranks of those about to be bronzed in print by Tracy Gilmartin.

"The evil!" declared Gusty, rising to his full five foot eight inches. His campaign manager heaved a sigh and waited for the biblical wrath to simmer down to political realism.

"Winston," he said, "do you now or have you ever had a bottle of Southern Comfort in your desk drawer?"

Gusty looked into the cynical eye of Willie Link, and his face twitched a little.

Willie nodded. "It's no sin," he said, and winced as Gusty let loose with one of his famous cries from the mountain in which he invoked the name of the Lord God and anyone else he thought might be of assistance.

"But of course it is a sin! The shame of it! I have sinned, Willie! Sinned!"

"Shhhh," said Willie, who knew how many reporters were outside. "You want to announce that in a press conference, Winston, or just have them hear it through the door?"

Gusty's blazing blue eyes narrowed. "A press conference," he said, and his voice became sonorous. "I shall admit my sin at a press conference. I shall beg the forgiveness of the electorate. Of my future constituents. Of the millions who have faith in me. Of my God."

"Very nice," said Willie, "but don't overdo it. All the column says is that she had a drink with you a while back."

"That's enough!" cried Gusty.

"It could be a lot worse," said Willie, who suspected it was.

"For me," said Gusty, "one sin is too many. I must be like Caesar's wife. You know that, Willie."

"What I know," Willie countered, "is that being human isn't going to hurt you with the voters. How many of them do you think haven't taken a snort or two? Even the ones who don't drink."

"How do you see the damage?" Gusty asked in his normal voice.

Willie shrugged. "You'll get the usual press caterwauling about hypocrisy and religious loonies, but you've gone through that before, and the polls show it doesn't matter like it used to. Remember Pat Robertson came right out and said okay, he did sleep with his wife before they were married, and the general reaction was what the hell, so had most of the voting public. You admit you've taken a drink and repented the wickedness of it, and nobody'll remember it next week except columnists who can't think of anything else to write. Get yourself revved up and go tell it on the podium, Winston."

Gusty looked at him with faint distaste. He respected and

valued Willie's expertise as a campaign manager, but he winced at his materialism and unabashed cynicism. He tried to keep Willie under wraps as much as possible, which suited the manager, who got more work done when he didn't have to keep explaining things to reporters.

"Where's Louis?" Gusty asked. As though on cue, the door opened and Louis Winant, a tall, handsome man who had been born in Haiti and had come to the United States as a teenager, entered. He wore an expression of outrage, and Willie sighed. Louis was devoted to Gusty to the point of fanaticism, in Willie's opinion, and he didn't think fanatics should be allowed in a well-run campaign. But Gusty needed a Louis to feed an ego of massive proportions. He couldn't fool Willie, and was shrewd enough to realize he shouldn't try to, but he couldn't do anything wrong where Louis was concerned. He reveled in his aide's hero worship.

"Winston! How dare they?" cried Louis, his face a wrathful mask of shining ebony. Gusty put his hand to his eyes, and Willie lit a cigarette.

"Louis"—Gusty held up a hand to silence the press secretary's expressions of sympathy—"I have sinned. I must tell the truth."

Louis was briefly taken aback.

"Winston means he did take a drink or two, and he's going to have a press conference and admit it," translated Willie, who had work to do and didn't have time to wait while the niceties were observed.

"I must tell the truth to my people," said Gusty in a vibrant purr.

Louis bowed his head.

"Try not to lose faith in me, Louis," Gusty implored him. "You know how much I need you, depend on you."

Louis clasped his hands. "I shall pray for you, Winston," he said.

"And get out the press release," Willie interjected.

"We must be strong under this burden. I know I have failed you, Louis. But I am frail in the eyes of the Lord," said Gusty.

Louis abruptly shook his head. "No—I am stunned by your strength in this adversity, Winston. We shall overcome."

Willie supposed that was going to be in the press release, but he didn't care. The *Spy* item might ultimately garner some points in the polls. Gusty could do worse than turn out to be human. Willie had always thought those angel's wings at the podium were overdoing it. This brought him down to earth, and a broken wing might be put to good use. He wondered about the *Spy* item.

"You knew this Gilmartin woman?" he asked, blowing a cloud of cigarette smoke between the bowed heads of Gusty and Winant.

"She helped in my campaign last year, as I recall. Or her mother did." Gusty's face was impassive.

"She's a dish, I hear," Willie noted, ignoring Louis's gesture of protest.

"I'm afraid I have no recollection of her appearance."

"Ahuh," said Willie.

"She must be *evil,*" Louis warned. "She seeks to bring down the messenger of the Lord."

Willie sighed. He sometimes thought that if Louis had stayed in Haiti, he would have been up to his elbows in voodoo. He overreacted to everything. "They're just tryin' to sell the book, Louis. Don't worry about it," he said soothingly. "Winston goes out there and tells it like it is, and this'll be no problem at all. May do us some good."

"No good can come of evil," Louis said. Willie supposed he should be grateful Louis had managed to restrain his religious fervor enough to talk like a normal human being in front of the press, most of whom thought he was a stitch.

"I suppose," said Gusty bitterly, as he combed his hair

before facing the lions of the fourth estate, "the Potterites will make the most of this."

"Of course they will," Willie said cheerfully. "It's all part of the game, Winston. Don't take it too seriously."

Joy was not unconfined in the White House, where the presidential pleasure over the revelation that the Reverend Winston Gusty had a weakness for Southern Comfort was considerably diluted by the source of the *Spy* item. The Potters looked at each other gloomily across the breakfast table.

"She's back," said the First Lady.

"What happened to Dim?" the President asked.

Linda sighed. "God knows. Last I heard—and Jayne's been keeping tabs on it because her housekeeper knows Dim's butler—they practically never got out of bed, and he was happy as a lark, laughing all the time."

"Laughing?"

"Well, I suppose they were enjoying themselves. Tracy's an entertaining woman, Sam. Among other things."

"But the plan didn't work."

"We don't know that. I mean, I didn't exactly expect them to elope," said Linda, who had been hoping for just that.

"The point is that she's back with Clapper. Writing that book."

"Well, at least she's bipartisan." Linda tried to see the bright side. She received no answering smile from her husband, who was staring at his congealing egg.

"Tell you what," she said. "I could have a word with Ken."

"Ken Singleton?" Potter stared at his wife. "Why would you want to talk to the director of the CIA about Tracy's book, for Christ's sake?" He drank his cold coffee and grimaced.

"Ken is a very resourceful man. And an old friend of ours," she pointed out.

The President heaved himself out of his chair, looking at his watch.

"Keep in mind," he said, "that assassination is illegal in this country."

"I know that," Linda replied. "Why would you bring it up?"

Chapter Ten

Benny Benton's jaws provided the only movement in a face that seemed to have been hewn out of charred wood. Throughout the flight, he had chewed constantly on sticks of Wrigley's Doublemint gum, his favorite. An offer of a snack of refreshments from a flight attendant brought only a grunt, not even a glance from his black button eyes. At Washington National Airport, he ground out a guttural phrase or two in order to pick up a rental car. Then he drove to a fast-food outlet to get a hamburger with cheese, onions, and pickles, which was hard on him, because it meant he had to temporarily lodge the gum behind a tooth. With his first bite, he poked two fingers into his mouth to disentangle the gum from the bun. He ate quickly, drank a large Coke, replaced his gum, and got back into the car. He drove around Cleveland Park for a while, consulting a hand-drawn street map on which one house was carefully marked. He checked his watch, drove around for a while longer, then made another swing down Roxbury Street as dusk began to fall and a light rain freckled his windshield.

He fidgeted in the driver's seat. He was tired. He thought

he had retired. But when Francis called for a favor, Benny had no choice. As that silly movie put it, it was an offer he couldn't refuse, if he wanted to continue receiving the comfortable percentage of the profits from the loanshark business that constituted his lavish pension.

This was, Francis assured him, a snap. And there would be a little bonus of a Caribbean vacation for him and Cissy. Benny sighed and turned on the car heater. The chill roused twinges in his arthritic ankle and the dampness irritated his sinus. He rubbed his leg, yawned, and dozed off for a few moments after parking in a cul-de-sac. He had to be careful about attracting any attention in the kind of neighborhood where people noticed strangers. Not that he was committing any crime. Just driving around a bit. But he was accustomed to a nap in the afternoon nowadays, and he missed it. His eyelids drooped, and when he woke himself up with his own snore, he realized he'd almost missed her.

She was scurrying down the paved path from the front door that led to the garage, and he noticed she seemed to be a little wobbly. Probably because of those crazy-looking shoes she was wearing. They made her look like she was on stilts. That thought flickered through his mind as he accelerated. Swinging the car hard right and putting his foot down in a burst of speed, he headed fast and straight for the dark green garage door at the moment she fumbled for its lock.

What happened next was a blur in his memory. He thought he'd got her. She'd seemed to flash across his line of vision and tumble to one side the way they usually did. But his reflexes weren't what they'd been in the old days, he was out of practice, and what with his aching ankle, his foot stayed too long on the gas. Next thing he knew was the sound of splintering wood and glass as the car slammed through the garage door and Benny's head slammed into the windshield.

Tracy told neighbors and the police it was the first time in her life she had ever been grateful for the kind of shoes she couldn't walk in. Sitting in her living room sipping hot coffee while a police officer took down details of the accident after Benny was carted off in an ambulance, Tracy kept going back to the shoes.

"I've always loved those crazy slingbacks, but those heels were just impossible. I mean, there was no *shoe* really. I could hardly stand, let alone walk, but they looked so terrific in the store mirror and they were exactly the right shade of blue. You know how hard it is to find something in the right spectrum of color, that isn't just a dull old match for what you're wearing."

"Mrs. Gilmartin," the policeman said patiently, "just try to tell me exactly what happened."

"I'm sorry," Tracy responded, flashing a smile that made him wonder why anybody would try to pound her into a garage door, assuming that was what had occurred.

"Well, I was in a hurry because I was going to drive over to Clayton Clapper's house for dinner. I'd had a late lunch date with Eleanor and then I did some shopping and I was running a little late. I hate to take my car downtown, so I'd taken metro in and got a cab back. Then I ran into the house for my diaries—"

"Eleanor?" the policeman asked.

"Eleanor McClusky, the senator. Illinois. We're old friends."

He made a note.

"Anyway, I really meant to change my shoes, but then I thought Clayton'd enjoy them because he thinks my clothes are crazy, so I kept them on. Then when I dashed out to the garage to get the car, my right heel caught in the crack between the lawn and the path, and I lost my balance and fell over. That was when the car just went roaring past me—it was so close it brushed my sleeve. I just sat there on the lawn and watched it smash right through my garage door. The car, I mean. I don't know what in the world he thought he was doing. He must have been drunk or something."

"Hmmmm," said the policeman, hoping he would be able to make sense of his notes.

"Did you talk to him—the driver?" Tracy asked, sticking a soothing finger into the cage of Chirp the canary, which was fussing because she had Benjamin the cat on her lap, and that put his claws closer than the bird liked.

Chirp and Benjamin were recent acquisitions. Tracy had decided to bring some life into her empty house. She knew where Tommy was, but she was uncertain where Rosemarie was, although she was afraid she knew. Chirp and Benjamin had become available because some neighbors were moving across country to an apartment complex where pets were frowned on. The neighbors warned her that probably the only thing that had kept Benjamin, large, gray and carnaptious, alive past his thirteenth year was his undying hope that one day he would succeed in his ambition to have Chirp for dinner. Tracy had been trying to teach the cat and the bird to live in harmony, but all her efforts had got her so far was a contemptuous stare from Benjamin and hysterics from Chirp.

"He's unconscious," the policeman said in response to her question about the driver of the car still wedged into her garage.

"Who is he?"

"Driver's license says Benjamin Benton of Chicago."

"How funny! He has the same name as my cat. From Chicago? Wait'll I tell Eleanor. Maybe he's a constituent." Tracy giggled a little shakily.

Joyce Willard, her neighbor, patted her shoulder soothingly. "Shouldn't you lie down or something?"

Tracy grimaced. "What I should do is take off these shoes. I might have twisted my ankle when I slipped. I mean, those shoes are dangerous. Why do they let them make things like that?" She caught the policeman's expression, and grinned. "Okay, I know. I'm crazy."

He found himself grinning back.

The telephone rang, and Tracy reached for it. "Clayton? I'm sorry, I'm sorry. But you'll never believe what just happened to me— What? You were? My God, how awful! When? What did they take?" She listened for a few moments. "I'll be over as soon as I can," she said. "I have this nice police officer here and— What? Oh, somebody drove his car right through my garage door. Damnedest thing you ever saw. Just missed *me,* as a matter of fact, and all because of those silly shoes, you know the ones with the slingbacks—"

The policeman closed his notebook as she launched into her shoe recital. When she put the telephone receiver down, Tracy looked excitedly at her audience.

"Clayton's house was burgled this afternoon! They stole his computer! And his tapes! Or our tapes, I should say. He said he just went to the market to get something for our dinner and they must have been watching, because when he came back, there wasn't a sign of a broken lock or anything, but the computer was gone, and some blank tapes he had on top of his desk. My *God!*"

She put her stockinged feet up on the coffee table.

Benjamin leapt to her shoulder, and Chirp uttered a squawk of alarm. Tracy put the huge gray cat on the floor and shook her finger at him. "Chirp is your friend," she said severely. Benjamin hissed at her.

"Where does your friend—Clayton, is it?—live?" the policeman asked.

"Georgetown. He has a townhouse with a nice little terrace outside his home office. He thinks that's how they got in, because there's a glass door and the lock isn't much. But at least they didn't damage anything." Tracy sighed. "I guess we've both been lucky today—sort of," she said.

The policeman hoped that if he were assigned to check

out the Georgetown robbery, Clayton would be a little less verbal about it. She was very attractive, but she talked as if she'd just abandoned a vow of silence. He checked what seemed to be pertinent information and took his leave.

Tracy picked up the phone again. "Eleanor?" she said. "You can't *imagine* what just happened!"

She told her, with emphasis on the subject of the shoes. Eleanor expressed horror and concern.

"I'm fine," Tracy assured her. "I don't know about the driver, though. I suppose he was drunk or stoned. He's unconscious, the police said. And you know, he's from Chicago?"

"Who is?"

"The man who drove his car through my garage door. His name was Benjamin. Isn't that funny, just like my new cat Benjamin? Benjamin Benton, wasn't that what the police officer said, Joyce?"

In Eleanor McClusky's head, a distant bell seemed to ring. She shivered convulsively. "Tracy, are you sure you're all right?"

"Absolutely. The car never touched me. I'm going over to Clayton's now because he's really upset. He got burgled this afternoon. Somebody stole his computer and his tapes."

"Clayton Clapper's house was robbed?"

"While you and I were having lunch, I guess."

Eleanor pawed in her desk drawer for aspirin, and noticed two message slips bearing reminders that her Uncle Francis had called from Chicago. She felt queasy and tried unsuccessfully to ignore her rising suspicion.

Tracy's voice was clear and cheerful. She had been so friendly and happy during their lunch that Eleanor could not read evil intent in those shining blue eyes. She could not bring herself to mention the book. Tracy had mentioned it, jokingly, saying she was flattered that any publisher would think she could write a social history of Washington. She added, shyly, she hoped Eleanor would do a blurb for the jacket when it came out. That had given Eleanor hope. Tracy certainly wouldn't be likely to ask her to praise a book in which she was being pilloried. Perhaps it really was a lighthearted book about parties and everyone was overreacting.

Eleanor let herself enjoy looking at Tracy and laugh at her description of how she kept falling off her shoes but they were so pretty she couldn't resist them and look at what they did for her legs. Eleanor noticed Tracy talked more than she used to; maybe that was the influence of writing. Her only bad moment came when Tracy flung her arms around her to say good-bye and kissed her on the cheek. Eleanor had felt herself go rigid.

"Take care of yourself, Tracy," she'd said, and fled. Now, on the telephone, she gave her the same advice, with more urgency.

Tracy hung up the phone, and winced as she rose from her chair, rubbing her ankle.

"For God's sake, put on other shoes," said her neighbor, who was preparing to leave and get on her phone so she could tell the neighborhood about the day's events. "How's your book coming?" she asked. "I read those little teasers in the gossip columns. Sounds like fun!"

"Oh, it is," said Tracy. "I still can't believe it, but my editor is very pleased, and Clayton says he's made a lot of progress with the writing. Just as well, because they want something by the end of next week, for planning purposes. They've already got plans for promotion! Talk shows and stuff like that!"

Joyce smiled at Tracy's enthusiasm. She liked Tracy, a kind and considerate neighbor who minded her own business, but was always willing to pour a cup of coffee or a glass of wine and let you sit down and tell her how the washer had broken down or your kid was on pot.

Joyce hoped Tracy would make a lot of money from her

book. Her husband had given Tracy a raw deal in Joyce's opinion, and Tracy hadn't said much about it. She hadn't even complained about him, which in Joyce's view qualified her for canonization. She'd been a little surprised, she had to admit, that Tracy was writing a book, but it just showed you couldn't judge by someone's appearance what was in her head.

Clayton Clapper was nervous. His feeling that a lot of people were unhappy about Tracy's book and that Jerry was overdoing the teasers had been confirmed. He had no doubt about what the burglars were after in his house and he didn't share Tracy's cheerful reaction to the demolition of her garage door and her own narrow escape. When she arrived, limping slightly, he was relieved she wasn't announcing she'd never write another word.

"Isn't it odd, such things happening to both of us on the same day?" she wondered.

"Well, things may be heating up a bit," Clayton said carefully.

"I don't understand. You think they're related? Your burglary and my garage door? That was probably just some drunk!"

"Maybe, maybe. But it's odd they stole only the computer and the tapes. I mean, there's the stereo and the VCR and the television."

"You think they were after the tapes?"

"Possible."

"But why? I've told everybody that what I'm writing is a social history! Why would that upset them? I'll bet it's those silly gossip items Jerry keeps handing out. It's giving an entirely wrong impression! Maybe we should tell him to stop it."

Clayton looked at Tracy's bewildered face and pondered the right thing to say. He couldn't risk her clamming up at this point. She was relaxed and rolling along with her stories, and she was translating her diaries without too much trouble.

There were still gaps, but he was beginning to put together a lively picture of Tracy's world. She was leaving the writing up to him because she trusted him. It was a peekaboo kind of social history, with all the warts left on its characters, because it was portrayed through the eyes of an observer who registered, remembered, and was now reporting what she'd seen when nobody noticed she was there.

Clayton had concluded that many of Tracy's friends and acquaintances had treated her as a sounding board, operating under the impression that talking to her was like talking to yourself. So far, he'd been careful about what segments he let Tracy read after he'd punched them into his computer. She was still jumpy about writing anything that would hurt people's feelings, as she put it, and there was a gathering mass of material that was simply juicy gossip. Kennally had read it with whoops of laughter, but Tracy hadn't read it at all.

Clayton had discussed with Kennally the possibility that Tracy would object to how the manuscript turned out. Their theory and their hope was that by then, she could hardly turn around and deny her own testimony, and, more important, she would be caught up in the excitement of publication, as well as the consolation of a large sum of money. It was a gamble they were prepared to take.

Clayton was fond of Tracy and he didn't want to hurt her. He also didn't want her to be hurt, and the incident with the garage door chilled him. Maybe Kennally was overdoing the gossip items, especially as it was unlikely that some of Tracy's most lurid pieces of scandal would get into print. Tracy was rarely stubborn, preferring to please everybody, but he'd learned to recognize what she wouldn't do.

Fortunately, she had a wealth of material she thought

was funny, and she saw no reason why she couldn't entertain readers. She loved to prattle about events at which prominent figures made themselves look silly and she had a good eye for idiosyncrasies, as evidenced by her story of the distinguished senator who unobtrusively clipped his fingernails in church because, he explained, he got bored when somebody else was talking.

But she drew the line at what she considered betrayal. She'd said flatly there was not to be a line in the book about Sam or Vladimir and she was sorry she'd joked about them, because it wasn't kind. Clayton wasn't certain they could persuade her otherwise. He was not without scruples, although increasingly they were tailored to his determination to fatten his bank balance and expand his reputation, but he knew there were few lines Mortimer and Kennally were unwilling to cross in the interests of mass circulation.

Tracy was looking at him worriedly. She hated people to think she had betrayed their trust in her. He smiled at her reassuringly.

"Don't worry. I'll talk to Jerry. Right now I've got some nice sole for dinner. I'll poach it."

She relaxed and began to paw through her diaries, curledin her favorite corner of the sofa, under the bookshelves.

"We were talking yesterday," said Clayton, "about that time you sat up all night with Charley Dill and he was discussing assassination . . ."

Tracy nodded. "That was fascinating. He was sort of philosophizing about intelligence work and that was about the time"—she riffled through pages—"there had been all the terrorism and then that awful man in the Middle East was shot . . ." She paused, fidgeting. "Clayton, I do feel a little edgy, I don't know why. Would you mind if we turned on some music while we talk?"

"Of course! And no wonder you're edgy. That idiot might have killed you this afternoon." He turned on the stereo and *The Ride of the Valkyries* filled the room. "Not very soothing, I'm afraid," he apologized.

"Oh, no, I love it!" Tracy exclaimed. "It makes me feel energetic!"

He laughed. "Let me get you a small sherry. That usually relaxes you."

Three blocks away, two men in a rented apartment frowned as they listened to what was filtering through the listening device placed that day in Clayton Clapper's house.

"Goddamn," said one of the listeners.

"Did it catch anything after 'shot'?"

"It caught Charley Dill talking about assassination," said the other, "and 'that awful man in the Middle East.' "

"But she said he was philosophizing about it."

"That," said the first man tersely, "is not how it will come out."

Chapter Eleven

"What do you mean, her cat was poisoned?" the First Lady asked. She was impatient about being called back to the telephone when she was on her way out the door to lunch. "Why should I care if Tracy's cat is dead? I didn't even know she had a cat."

Jayne Millspaw's voice was low and urgent, the way she sounded when she had a juicy piece of gossip to impart. "I just talked to Tracy. No, I called her. I thought *somebody* should ask her how her book's going. I thought you'd certainly want to keep track, darling. So anyway I called and she was in hysterics. She thinks somebody's trying to kill her."

"What makes her think that?" Linda asked, but refrained from observing that the thought might have crossed the minds of more than one person in the past few weeks.

"Well." Linda sat down. She wasn't often late to lunch, but she could plead urgent official business to the president of the League of Women Voters once she got to the restaurant.

"Last week," Jayne related with relish, "she told me somebody drove his car through her garage door just as she was about to open it. He missed her because she fell off the heel of one of her shoes or something and was in a heap on the lawn when the car went smashing into her garage. She wasn't hurt or anything, but when she stopped explaining how grateful she was that she wore crazy shoes, she sounded shaken up."

"Who was driving the car? I didn't see anything about it in the papers."

"Somebody from Chicago. He's in the hospital with a concussion. He told the police he'd had a seizure and lost control of the car. At the time, Tracy said she didn't think that much about it. Then the cat dropped dead."

Linda sighed. "So the cat dropped dead."

"She just got the cat and it liked to be walked on a leash. It was an old cat, she said, about as big as a horse, practically. She was taking it to the vet on Seventeenth Street and she said there was a crowd of people around her. The cat's leash got tangled, so it was sort of wrapped around her leg, the cat, I mean, and then it collapsed. She thought it'd had a stroke or something, and rushed it to the vet's office and sure enough it was dead. He couldn't figure out what it died of and Tracy was upset because the cat had belonged to her neighbors who'd moved, so she had them do an autopsy. And it turned out it had been poisoned! A poisoned dart!" Jayne's voice was sibilant with melodrama.

"Well—that's awful, but I still don't see—"

"Tracy told me she's terrified! She thinks the cat got the dart that was meant for *her* ankle and instead wound up in its hind paw!"

"Jesus Christ!" Linda exclaimed.

"Isn't that *fascinating*?" said Jayne.

"It's—it's terrible, I mean, if it's true," Linda replied uneasily. "Who'd want to kill Tracy?"

"Come *on*," Jayne told her. "You could probably count them on the fingers of both hands, dear."

"Jayne," said Linda, "This isn't funny. I mean, what if she's right?"

"What if she's right?"

"This is murder!"

"That's the way a lot of people seem to feel about that book," Jayne pointed out.

"Nobody would—"

"You heard about Clayton Clapper's house being burgled?"

Linda hesitated.

"Well, yes."

"And all they took was his computer."

Linda was silent.

"I can't wait for the *Post* to get its claws on this," said Jayne.

Linda thought she could wait forever.

"Has there been anything at all in the papers so far?"

"Not a line. But if Tracy starts to announce in public that she's the target of assassins because she's writing a book about Washington high jinks, or low jinks, however you want to look at it, she's going to be all over page one, not to mention television."

"Oh, *God,*" said Linda. She wondered how she could spend the next hour discussing the need for increasing political female activity at the grass-roots level.

"I knew you'd want to know," said Jayne. "I hope I didn't interrupt anything. I'll keep you posted."

She sounded positively elated, Linda thought. She reflected, not for the first time, that Jayne was an awful person. Tracy, she thought bitterly, was much nicer. She became aware that her press secretary was hovering in the doorway.

"The car is ready, Mrs. Potter."

"Susie," said Linda with sudden decision, "you'll have to call Joan Kipper at the restaurant. Something important's come up and I just can't make it. Or wait, I tell you what, go over there and have lunch with her. Slather her with apologies and invite her to have lunch with me here at the White House next week. She'll like that."

Susie looked confused. "Is—something wrong?" she asked.

Linda smiled at her conspiratorially. "Just a personal problem, but I have to attend to it. I just can't concentrate on grass-roots politics right now."

Susie smiled understandingly.

"Take the car. It'll be faster," said the First Lady, "and give Joan a ride back to her office."

She closed the door to the family sitting room, picked up the phone, and dialed a private line that was scrambled to protect its security. "Ken? This is Linda Potter."

The director of the Central Intelligence Agency blinked. "Linda. How are you?"

"Fine. I need to talk to you for a minute or two."

"Of course." There wasn't much else he could say to the President's wife.

"You know we talked the other day about the Tracy Gilmartin matter."

"Yes." Ken Singleton's voice was cautious. He'd told Linda Potter, politely but firmly, that he thought people were overreacting to what was likely to be a very trivial book, and that under no circumstances would he allow the agency, while he was running it, to become involved in anything like that. He reminded her of what had happened to Richard Nixon when he sought to make illegal domestic use of the CIA. He also made clear that his fondness for her and for the President, who had appointed him to the job, would not influence him to the point of presiding over another disaster at Langley. He'd heard that the director of the FBI had arranged some assistance, to the point of bugging the telephone of Gilmartin's ghostwriter, Clayton Clapper. He hadn't approved of that, either.

"Something else has come up," said Linda. She related

what she'd been told by Jayne Millspaw. Singleton listened with impatience at first, then with a faint frown.

"Is this possible?" Linda asked.

"You mean the cat business being aimed at her? I suppose it is."

"How do you shoot darts in the middle of Seventeenth Street, for God's sake?"

"Well, I don't know whether that was done, but there have been instances where the tip of an umbrella was used to jab the ankle of a target."

"Then it sounds like it, doesn't it?"

"It sounds odd," he agreed, "but I still think you're dramatizing this, Linda."

"But the cat thing's coming on top of somebody trying to mash her into a garage door last week, Ken!"

"It does seem a strange coincidence, I'll grant you that."

"I mean, I know people are upset. But nobody wants to kill her." Linda's voice had risen a notch, he noticed.

"I wouldn't think so. But given the fact that you are so concerned about this, others may be even more so. Whether it's justified or not." He hesitated. "Has Tracy been—ah—playing around with any of the diplomatic people, as far as you know?"

"I don't know. I wouldn't be surprised, though."

"Well, it's hard to tell. They may be overreacting, too."

"Why are you so sure *we're* overreacting?"

"Well, what you're basing your concern on are a few gossip items. Only those involved know what she could tell. They may be no more than teasers."

"We can't afford to take that risk."

Singleton's eyebrows rose. "I gather she has something on you? And on Sam?"

"I really don't know about Sam," said Linda slowly. "Maybe he screwed her some time. I mean, apparently just about everybody else has. But—well, she and I used to tell each other a lot of stuff."

"About men."

"Yes."

"Why would she write about that?"

"I wish I knew. But you know how the public is about morality among politicians nowadays. I mean, Sam's got a campaign coming up."

"I'm aware of the political fallout that could result. But look at what happened after Winston Gusty held that press conference confessing the sin of consuming a little Southern Comfort after a long campaign day. He went up in the polls, according to what I'm told. People approved of his being honest enough to admit he wasn't perfect."

"He wouldn't have admitted it, if it had been any *more* serious," said Linda sourly.

"The point was that the public reaction showed a degree of common sense, even a sense of humor."

"I'm still worried."

"What did the bug come up with?"

There was a pause.

"How'd you know about that? Well, I suppose that is a foolish question, isn't it, Ken?"

"I'm supposed to know about things, even when I don't approve of them because I think they involve unnecessary political risk."

Linda ignored the reproof. "Ken, come off it. We've known each other for years. We're not trying to get your beloved Company involved."

The hell they weren't, thought Singleton, and waited for a reply to his question.

"Not much," she said wearily. "There was a reference to Charley Dill philosophizing about assassination. Then they turned on *The Ride of the Valkyries* on the stereo."

Singleton grinned.

"You think that was intentional?"

"Probably not," Linda admitted. "And Tracy didn't say Charley had done any more than philosophize, although she mentioned it was at the time 'that awful man in the Middle East' got killed, as she put it. That sounds like Tracy."

"Does Charley know?"

"He's not happy. And of course we don't know what else she's telling Clapper. Unfortunately, Charley can't remember what he told *her*."

Singleton rolled his eyes. "I still think this may be a tempest in a teapot," he told the First Lady in an infuriatingly cheerful voice. Linda resisted an impulse to hang up because she knew he might be right. Singleton was often right, usually when the conventional wisdom was that he was wrong.

"What if she starts telling the press somebody's trying to kill her?" she asked.

"The only comment anybody could make on that is that she's imagining things and she ought to be talking to the metropolitan police. She's not going to accuse you or the President. Is she?"

"Of course not. Don't be ridiculous. But if she did start giving interviews, it'd get that book of hers even more attention."

"That's probably true," said Singleton. However, he thought that the publishers of the Gilmartin book would want to keep her alive, at least until after publication day, and for that reason she would be unlikely to go public about her fears with their blessing. "Maybe what you ought to do is protect her," he said.

The subtlety was lost on Linda. "That will be a cold day in hell," she said. "Thanks a lot, Ken."

Singleton contemplated the receiver thoughtfully before replacing it. It was an interesting dilemma, because the First Lady could be right. Tracy Gilmartin might be a political time bomb set to explode in the middle of a presidential election year. He wondered about the cat. That sounded clumsy, but it had a certain professional ring to it. Certainly the Soviets were notoriously sensitive to scandal, implied or real. But *that* sensitive? Unless there was more to Tracy than anyone had suspected. He assumed the FBI had run a make on her because there wasn't much Joe Tibbits, the director, wouldn't do to please the President. But there were people around Washington who might know more than they had so far admitted about Tracy. Discreet inquiries could be made about that. And he'd like to know more about the autopsy on the cat.

Singleton picked up a newspaper file and flicked through the pages until he came to clippings about Winston Gusty's press conference, which sounded to him more entertaining than the writer had given it credit for. He noticed Willie Link, a veteran newsman turned political consultant, had joined Gusty's staff. That was an indication the evangelist might have more political smarts than Singleton had so far thought. The director of Central Intelligence had known Link for years, and had a high opinion of his political judgment, although he thought Willie might be backing the wrong horse this time around. Maybe he was bored with conventional politics.

He wondered how Willie got along with Louis Winant, who was generally considered a loose cannon, not to say a raving madman. For that matter, he wondered why someone as shrewd as Gusty would retain a high-visibility aide as unpredictable as Winant.

Which was a question being asked almost at that moment by Willie Link, who had discovered in a desk drawer—the lock of which he had jimmied in the belief that alcohol was concealed there—a doll. It was a crudely made thing, apparently carved from a soft clay, and it was clearly a female, with grotesquely exaggerated breasts and buttocks and a thatch of yellow hair. What caught Willie's attention was the distribution, at strategic points on the doll, of small steel pins.

"Jesus God," said Willie, and put the doll on the top of

the desk as though it were a toad. He reached into a pocket for his cigarettes and was smoking moodily, staring at the doll, when Winston Gusty walked into the room.

"What on earth is that?" Gusty demanded.

"You tell me," said Willie through a drift of smoke. "It was in the desk drawer." He looked up. "I found it because the drawer was locked, and being of a nasty, suspicious mind, I thought that meant it contained an alcoholic beverage."

"Where did it come from?" Gusty's face was contorted by distaste. He didn't touch the doll, for which Willie didn't blame him. It lay there, bristling and sinister.

"I'm damned if I know, Winston. It ain't mine. And I don't think it's yours. But this office is only used by the press staff."

Gusty's rugged face paled a little, and he sat down abruptly on top of a pile of releases stacked on a straight-backed chair on the other side of the desk.

"Willie," he said in a voice that came close to quavering. "You don't think—"

Willie lit another cigarette from the stub of the first, a habit he'd been trying to break, partly because it upset the candidate. "I don't know," he said in a tired voice. "But if I had to make an educated guess—"

"Dear God," Gusty said, and Willie reflected that he sounded genuinely prayerful.

"Why don't you ask him?" he suggested. Gusty shuddered slightly.

"Not Louis," he said miserably.

Willie picked up the phone. "Hey, Milly, is Winant down there? Tell him Winston wants to see him."

Gusty sat staring at the floor, and Willie felt sorry for him. First the Southern Comfort and now this. He suspected the candidate could use a little Southern Comfort right now.

"Winston," he said gently, "better you find out now."

Gusty nodded silently, stood up, and walked to the window, where he stood, his hands linked behind his back. It would make a nice campaign shot, Willie thought reflexively, sort of like that one of JFK standing at the White House window. Gusty was tall and well built, too, with a noble cast to his profile, and an excellent haircut.

Willie looked up as Louis Winant walked in with his usual confident stride and stopped dead in front of the desk. Winant's finely modeled face was stony. He glanced over at Gusty, who had not turned around. He said nothing.

Willie sighed and picked up the doll. "This yours, Louis?"

Winant made no move, letting Willie sit there with his hand outstretched, holding the doll. Willie supposed it was his imagination, but his hand felt numb, and he abruptly tossed the doll into a wastebasket beside the desk. Winant's eyes followed it, but he still did not speak.

"Louis," said Gusty's voice, but the candidate did not turn around.

Winant looked toward Gusty. "Winston," he said in an oddly hoarse voice. "The evil . . ."

Gusty turned and faced him. Willie thought the candidate had never looked better. It augured well for debates with his opponents if he was this dignified when he was mad. Gusty pointed with a thunderbolt finger to the thing in the wastebasket. "That is the evil," he said. "Louis, how could you do this to me?"

"I wanted—to protect you—" Winant's voice was a dismal whisper. Willie sighed. It was no comfort to him that his pessimistic gut feelings about Louis had proved accurate. Now he supposed he'd have to cope with the damned press without having Winant to throw to them to satisfy their craving for copy. He looked at Winant resentfully.

Gusty was still playing high priest to Winant's voodoo doll.

"You could have destroyed me totally. All we wanted to

do together. Our faith in what we wanted to do. Louis—you and I have *prayed* together!"

But probably not to the same God, thought Willie, stubbing out his cigarette in deference to the drama of the occasion.

Winant's head was bowed now. "Forgive me, Winston," he said. "I did it for you."

Gusty nodded solemnly and held out his hand. "You knew not what you did, Louis," he said in a voice that seemed to roll around the room. "Go and sin no more."

Winant clasped Gusty's hand, and Willie saw tears streak the black cheeks.

"I shall go to church," he said softly, "and pray for forgiveness. And for you, Winston. For your success as the savior of this land."

Gusty's face softened. At last Winant had said the right thing, Willie reflected. He put his other hand over Winant's and patted it. He was still standing very erect, his head high. Willie nodded approvingly, then stirred uneasily as Winant raised his eyes imploringly to Gusty's face.

"If I repent—if I have your forgiveness—then can I—come home?"

Willie realized he needn't have worried, because Gusty didn't hesitate. His expression was solemn but gentle, his voice almost tender, but his words were clear and firm.

"Go back to our church in Alabama, Louis. Back to our roots. Cleanse your soul of this"—his eyes flickered to the wastebasket and Winant winced—"this obscenity. Perhaps then—and by then, we hope we shall have triumphed in our cause—then we may talk again. But not for a while, Louis. You have disappointed me—no, hurt me—deeply."

He withdrew his hand from Winant's grasp and walked back to the window. Winant stood for a moment staring at the candidate's well-tailored back. Briefly, he glanced toward Willie, who raised a hand.

"See you, Louis," he said, and watched Winant's dejected departure. Gusty turned around almost immediately.

"Willie," he said, "can you believe this kind of thing?"

"Frankly, no. It surprised even me. But you bring out this kind of devotion in people, Winston," Willie told him. "Let's hope you have the same effect on the voters. As I said, let's be grateful it happened now, and not later. I mean, voodoo in the Oval Office? Voodoo economics are one thing, but voodoo dolls?"

Gusty peered at it. "You'll get rid of that thing?"

"I'm sure as hell not going to leave it around." Willie fished the doll out by its yellow hair and dumped it in a brown paper bag.

"The incinerator. Not the trash can," said Gusty.

Willie grinned, and nodded. Then he paused. "Hey, I wonder how she's feeling?" he said.

Chapter Twelve

The Clean Sweep Company arrived on Roxbury Street in a white van that carried two men wearing white uniforms and broad smiles. Howie, who was the spokesman, with George beaming over his shoulder, explained they were demonstrating a revolutionary new method of cleaning chimneys.

"No fuss, no muss. You don't even know we're there," as he put it. It was all done by ultrasonic waves, all very high-tech, and it even disinfected the chimney in addition to removing the soot, he said with a dazzling display of teeth. It was free, because they wanted to prove what they could do, then offer contract deals to satisfied customers.

"They loved us in New York and Miami," said Howie, "so we're expanding into the Washington and Maryland area. And no charge at all for our first treatment of your chimney. No need for us even to enter the house, as a matter of fact. It's a brand-new process. Try us. If you don't like how your fire burns after we've done your chimney, call our eight-hundred number and we'll do it again."

He distributed cards. All the houses on Roxbury Street had at least one chimney, and all the householders subjected to the earnest but amiable persuasion of Howie and George accepted the offer. All except Joyce Willard, who had been brought up to believe you didn't get something for nothing, and if it sounded too good to be true, it probably was. Not that Howie was aggressive, she had to concede that. He made her feel a little surly by reacting philosophically to her rejection of his offer.

"Entirely up to you, Mrs. Willard," he said. "We never pressure people, because people who are pressured aren't comfortable customers. Maybe you should wait and see how your neighbors like our service. Just let me give you our card."

Joyce smiled at him apologetically. "I'm sure you do fine work," she assured him, "but I just had my chimney done and—well, maybe I'll call you. I'll keep your card."

"That's all we ask," said Howie. "Maybe you'll give us a call in a month or two."

"I'll certainly keep you in mind."

"Mrs. Brown, three doors up, was delighted," said George, who looked too large for his white uniform. Joyce nodded again, and turned back into her house.

"By the way,"said Howie. "We've tried to catch Mrs. Gilmartin next door a couple of times. Is she away, or could we leave a card with you for her?"

"Her maid's there today," said Joyce. "You could check with her."

Howie nodded his thanks. From her window, Joyce saw Howie and George ring Tracy's doorbell. Ella Mae, the twice-weekly cleaning woman, appeared, wearing the expression she reserved for people trying to sell her something. On being assured that Clean Sweep wanted only to offer a free trial that didn't involve their setting foot over the threshold, but required only the insertion of a device into the top of the chimney, Ella became less belligerent. Tracy wasn't home, but as long as it didn't cost anything, and they'd been working at houses up and down the street (she'd seen them), she didn't think it could hurt to let them try it, as long as she kept an eye on them. Which she did, standing with their arms folded while they climbed a metal folding ladder onto the roof and capped the chimney with what looked like a box wrapped in aluminum foil. That, Howie explained, was the container for the ultrasonic sweep.

Ella waited until they climbed down, in case they fell through the roof, as she said to herself. Howie gave her their card and urged her to have Mrs. Gilmartin call as soon as she had lit a fire in the sitting room, to report on the improvement. Ella put the card on the coffee table in the sitting room and forgot to mention it to Tracy.

The card, charred around the edges, survived the explosion that shook the house and wrecked the sitting room when Tracy felt chilly and lit a fire that evening. Tracy, who had gone upstairs immediately after starting the fire in the grate, thought it was an earthquake at first. Then she went downstairs and found the door blown out of the sitting room and chaos within.

The destruction of the room was bad enough, but what reduced Tracy to hysterical tears was Chirp. His cage had been catapulted across the room by the blast, and unfortunately the canary had been poking his head between the bars at the time, which led to his decapitation.

Tracy stared at the ruined room, littered with shards of glass from the broken windows as well as her best crystal from what was once an elegant mahogany corner cupboard. Chirp's headless corpse was on the bottom of what was left of his cage, and she didn't want to know where the rest of him was. Helplessly, she sat down on the stairs, unable to move. It wasn't until she heard sirens outside that she staggered to the front door and opened it to admit what looked like a cast of thousands. There were firemen, police, and neighbors led by Joyce Willard, wailing that she knew it, she *knew* they weren't chimney sweeps.

Tracy could only stare at them. Suddenly, she wanted to talk to Tommy. She'd never had a crisis when he wasn't there. Although, come to think of it, she'd never had this kind of crisis before.

"I have to call my husband," she told a police officer who looked familiar. She realized he was familiar because he'd interviewed her after that madman had driven a car through her garage door.

"Hello again," Tracy said, trying to smile.

The policeman shook his head. "Ma'am, you sure do have your problems," he commented mildly.

"I sure do," said Tracy. "I'll be right back." She went upstairs, clinging to the banister, and collapsed on her bed for a moment before she picked up the telephone and dialed the number Tommy had left with her. The voice that answered was not that of Tommy, and Tracy hesitated, then plunged on. After all, it *was* an emergency.

"This is Tracy Gilmartin," she said in as firm a voice as she could muster. "Is Tommy there?"

"He's asleep," the voice responded unhelpfully.

Tracy's rare temper flared. "Then would you wake him? Tell him his house in Washington's just been bombed."

"Bombed?" said the voice incredulously.

"That's what I said. B-O-M-B-E-D."

There was a lengthy silence before Tommy came on the line. He sounded cross. She remembered he had always been cross when he was waked from a nap.

"Tracy, what's going on?" He sounded incredulous.

Tracy was furious. What did she have to do to be taken seriously? Die? "I'll tell you what's going on," she said, willing her voice not to tremble. "Benjamin's been poisoned, Chirp's been beheaded, my garage door's smashed, and they just bombed the sitting room. *That's* what's going on."

"Tracy," said Tommy, "are you high on something? Who's Benjamin? Who's Chirp? Who's bombed the sitting room?"

"Benjamin was my cat and Chirp was my canary, and I don't know who bombed the sitting room or tried to squash me against the garage door with a car. That's what the police are downstairs trying to figure out."

"I don't understand any of this. I didn't know you *had* a cat or a canary."

"That isn't the point!" Tracy's voice rose. "Ever since I started writing my book, it's as though all hell's broken loose. I don't understand it! People don't seem to like me any more!"

"What book?"

"Oh, *God,*" said Tracy. "I'm writing a book. A social history of Washington. Or rather, Clayton Clapper's writing it for me. Wissip Golight is publishing it. I thought it would be a way to make some money."

She hiccuped softly, and there was a pause on the other end. Tommy Gilmartin was not an unkind man, and he felt guilty about Tracy, perhaps because he didn't want to live with her anymore.

"Listen, calm down. Try to tell me slowly. You're writing a book about Washington. What about?"

"I told you. It's a social history. Funny stories about parties I've been to, and social disasters. Political stuff that didn't come out before, that people told me. My own observations about people and things." That was one of Clayton's phrases.

"I never heard you make any observations. You occasionally told a funny story, but I always had the impression you were very close-mouthed, Tracy. I had to drag stuff out of you, if I needed information on a business contact who was a friend of yours. But now you're writing a book about all this? It doesn't sound like you."

"That's right," said Tracy coldly. "Because nobody ever listened to me before. Nobody thought I had anything to say. Not until now, Tommy. But my *editor* thinks I have a lot to say, and that a lot of people will pay to read it. And as I told you, I need money."

"I'll send you money."

"Don't bother. I can take care of myself. You have Raymond to look after," said Tracy with uncharacteristic venom.

"I still can't make head or tail of why people are trying to kill you," said Tommy, choosing to ignore her last remark.

"Well, there've been items in gossip columns, about how this is going to be a tell-all book. Of course, it isn't, really. But Jerry—that's my editor at WG—said it would help get people interested."

"He's obviously right," Tommy said dryly. "But they may be overdoing it."

Tracy suddenly felt drained. She wished she hadn't called Tommy. Listening to his voice made her remember he didn't care any more, and that made her feel worse, when she was feeling bad enough already. Nobody cared about her. People wanted her dead. She hung up the phone and burst into tears.

Joyce Willard, who had been hovering outside the door, with a backup team of neighbors and police, and an ambulance crew who had recently joined the throng, rushed in. Tracy wept on her shoulder while neighbors brought her a glass of water, cold cloths, and ran home for brandy, because the Gilmartin liquor supply was now distributed around the sitting room walls. The telephone rang. It was Tommy calling back, anxious about Tracy. She refused to talk to him.

"Ask her if she wants me to come to Washington," he told Joyce Willard, who was presiding with efficiency and a certain amount of relish over the continuing pandemonium. Joyce was a well-organized woman whose house and family were nowhere enough to keep her occupied. She was perfectly prepared to add Tracy's troubles to her responsibilities. It was the most excitement in sedate Roxbury Street in twenty years.

Joyce conveyed Tommy's message to Tracy, who sobbed harder. "She does not," said Joyce.

Tracy nodded tearful agreement. "T-tell him to go—go back to sleep with his damned Raymond," said Tracy.

Joyce told him. She hung up just before Tommy did.

It was a long night. In the wake of the police, the firemen, the paramedics, and a procession of worried and curious neighbors came the press. Joyce Willard was not displeased to be requested to speak for Tracy, who declaimed from the head of the stairs, "My pets have been killed, my house is a wreck, somebody's trying to murder me, and I don't know why. I never want to talk to anyone again."

It was, as one reporter observed, a quote that got things off to a promising start. Joyce was cooperative about filling them in on the garage crash, the murder of Benjamin the cat on Seventeenth Street, and the beheading of Chirp the parakeet in the bombed-out sitting room. Television lights illuminated the neighborhood, and cameras caught a dramatic shot of Tracy at an upstairs window with her hands to her face. The story made a nice package on the eleven o'clock news and in the Washington papers the next morning. In addition to a prominently displayed news story, the *Post* ran a lengthy piece in the Style section that was a combination of interviews of people who knew Tracy, and an analysis of what was dubbed "Tracygate." It suggested that the collective conscience of certain prominent people in the nation's capital had to be dark indeed if the threat of publicizing their peccadilloes led to attempted murder.

It was also discovered that the investigation of the strange happenings around the Gilmartin house was running into mysterious impediments. It surprised nobody that there was no such organization as the Clean Sweep Company. But that was followed by the disclosure that the remains of Benjamin the cat had disappeared, together with the report on the cause of his death, and Benny Benton had been spirited out of George Washington Hospital.

In the White House, President Potter read the paper, watched television, and groaned.

"What in hell is going on?" he asked his wife, who was alternating aspirin with white wine. She shook her head, and Potter looked at her suspiciously. "Did you talk to Ken Singleton again?" he demanded.

She was both indignant and bitter. "He was no help at all. Said we were overreacting and got pious about the agency not getting involved in this kind of thing. Brought up Nixon."

"Well, he's right," said her husband grudgingly. "They've got to watch their ass nowadays, Linda."

"What about our ass?" she asked tartly.

"Look," he said, "this is crazy stuff. Bombing, poisoning, attempted murder! For Christ's sake, Linda, who's after her? D'ya have any idea at all who's behind this? I hope to God you don't."

She shook her head. "Come on, Sam, the farthest I got was when the FBI did that little bugging for you, on grounds that national security might be compromised. You thought *that* was a good idea, didn't you?"

"Sort of. All they got was Wagner, so I don't know if it was worth the risk. But this whole business is ridiculous. Not only that, but it's rank incompetence, whoever's doing it!"

The private line rang and Linda jumped. Potter answered it.

"Mr. President," said Ken Singleton.

"I'm glad you called," said Potter.

"This Tracy Gilmartin business," said the DCI.

"We were just talking about it. You know anything about this uproar?"

"I know *nothing* about it," said Singleton. "That's why I'm calling. It's beginning to look as though the Soviets are after her."

He didn't mention that the Clean Sweep Company appeared to have been composed of Cuban mercenaries whose services had been utilized once or twice by the CIA before it discovered their reliability was dubious, their loyalty for hire, and their competence questionable.

"You mean the *Russians* are trying to kill her? Why, for Christ's sake?" Potter sputtered.

"The last attempt, and possibly the poisoning, when they got the cat. They've used that method before."

"But why? I mean, surely that damned book wouldn't justify this?"

"That's what we're wondering," said Singleton. "Could there be more to Tracy Gilmartin than anyone has realized?"

The CIA inquiries about Tracy had produced no results beyond that everybody already knew. Singleton had become intrigued as to whom the woman might be working for. Although, if she were an agent, why would she have got herself into this welter of lunatic publicity? As one of his assistants had observed that morning. "It sounds like Mata Hari and the Three Stooges."

"Ken," said the President, "I don't know a goddamn thing about any of this stuff. We—all we did—or the FBI did, as I'm sure you know—was a little—ah, security check of Clapper's place."

Singleton grinned. "I heard about that. But this has become genuinely puzzling."

"I want to tell you, between us," said the President with sudden ferocity, "I wish they'd been more efficient about it, whoever they are. I can't believe how much trouble that woman has caused."

Singleton refrained from pointing out that as far as he could tell, the trouble the President was talking about preoccupied the minds of the guilty.

"However, Mr. President," he said, "I trust the White House will continue to—"

"Keep as far removed from the whole thing as possible. You're goddamned right," Potter finished the sentence. "Thank God, we really *aren't* involved. I mean, we *can* deny it and not worry about it."

"I hear," Singleton mentioned, "that she isn't planning to go through with the book. So the story in the *Post* says, anyway."

"I read it. But I also noticed that sleaze Mortimer at Wissip Golight said no author of his would be muzzled by terrorists. Hell, he's on the talk shows. Mortimer the defender of the fourth estate. A goddamned slumlord."

"Yes, well," said Singleton, recognizing signs that the President was winding up for a tirade.

"Maybe what we're in is a holding pattern. As a matter of fact, apart from continuing to check out Gilmartin's background from an intelligence standpoint, there's nothing we can or should do. The whole thing is bizarre. None of our assets has been able to come up with anything helpful about the woman."

"All I want," said the President wearily, "is a normal campaign year. Let's hope this pattern, or whatever it is, holds until November so I can try to get reelected."

Chapter Thirteen

Tracy was on the telephone, arguing with her home insurance company that a bombing was not an act of God, when out of the corner of her eye, she saw the front door slowly begin to open. She put down the phone, picked up a brass candlestick from the hall table, and darted behind the door as it swung creakily open—it had creaked since the explosion—to admit her daughter, Rosemarie, bearing a black eye and carrying a suitcase. She stared open-mouthed at her mother and at the candlestick in her hand.

"Why are you creeping in here like that?" demanded Tracy, whose nerves were frayed.

Rosemarie, accustomed to warm welcomes, no matter how stormy her departure, looked taken aback.

"It wasn't locked," she said with unusual meekness.

Tracy put down the candlestick and hugged her daughter perfunctorily. She was in no mood to put up with Rosemarie, girl revolutionary.

"I'm glad to see you. But things are absolutely crazy around here."

Rosemarie put down her suitcase and peered around her in bewilderment. She stared through the sitting room doorway at the room, which was now stripped of most of its debris and awaiting repair.

"What have you been *doing?*" she asked.

"It isn't what *I've* been doing," her mother said. "It's what other people have been doing."

Tracy sighed. She was sick of reciting her catalog of catastrophes, although nobody seemed sick of hearing it, from the press to the police.

"Take your bag up to your room and I'll tell you about it," she said wearily. She looked more closely at her daughter's face. "What happened to your eye?" She had a feeling she already knew, and Rosemarie's sheepish expression confirmed it.

"He beat me."

"Jared?"

Rosemarie nodded. "You're not surprised, are you?" she asked with a trace of resentment.

Tracy shrugged. "What good would it have done to warn you?"

Rosemarie continued to stand there, clutching her suitcase, looking surprised. She was unaccustomed to a tough Tracy; she didn't know how to deal with it. Given past performance, her mother should have been rushing upstairs with her bag, making icepacks for her eye, exuding sympathy all the while. The level of maternal cosseting seemed to have plummeted during the weeks of Rosemarie's absence and she was uncertain how to cope with a Tracy who apparently had been prepared to hit her with a candlestick.

"He told me—that he'd known you a long time ago," she said with some of her old sullenness.

"True," said Tracy briskly. "I gather he hasn't changed. He was always a bomb thrower. If you'll pardon the expression." She glanced around her and winced.

Rosemarie put down her suitcase and gestured around. "What did happen here?"

"I need a cup of coffee," her mother said. "Let's go sit in the kitchen—nobody's blown *it* up yet—and I'll fill you in. For that matter, maybe you can fill me in too on just where *you've* been and what you've been up to."

Rosemarie followed her meekly and sat down in the round table in the sunny niche where Tracy and Tommy used to have breakfast.

"We have any fresh orange juice?" she asked.

Tracy shook her head. "I don't even know if we have oranges. You can look in the refrigerator," she. said, and poured two cups of strong coffee.

Rosemarie realized unhappily that the old Tracy who would have leapt for the oranges and the juicer was absent. She peered into the refrigerator. He mother was right. There were no oranges. There wasn't much of anything except some suspicious-looking cheese and a bottle of white wine. She'd never seen the refrigerator so desolate and her mother seemed to neither know nor care. She sat down and sipped the coffee, which almost stood her hair on end.

"Mother," she said politely, "will you please tell me what's going on?"

Tracy eyed her. She didn't much feel like telling the whole story from the beginning, and she was of the opinion that Rosemarie had some explaining of her own to do.

"Let's hear about our mutual revolutionary friend," she said, and was not surprised when Rosemarie began to cry. Tracy waited until the sobs had subsided, and offered her daughter a box of Kleenex.

"Nothing you say will surprise me, sweetie, so talk it out," she told her.

Rosemarie blew her nose. "He— It was awful," she said with a sniffle. Tracy waited.

"Practically from the beginning," Rosemarie went on, "he didn't seem to care that I'd given up everything to join him —to help the cause."

She paused to wipe away another tear with a soggy tissue and Tracy maintained an impassive expression while reflecting that she had a certain amount of empathy for Jared Filega as far as his reaction to Rosemarie's sacrifices was concerned.

"He—he told me I made too many speeches and he—he said I was a spoiled b-brat who didn't know what she was talking about. He said I was like all Americans—that I talked a lot and never said anything. I c-couldn't believe it. I mean, he'd told me he was dying to see me. He s-said I was his woman."

Tracy sighed and poured herself more coffee.

"Did he say all this before or after he went to bed with you?" she asked sadly.

Rosemarie choked and disappeared into another wad of Kleenex. "B-before."

Tracy patted her on the shoulder. "Happens to all of us, honey," she said. "You're entitled to make a mistake, you know."

"But I believed in him!" Rosemarie wailed. "I left home for him. I d-dropped out of school for him after I met him at that rally last May. He was so dedicated—I thought he was so dedicated."

"He is. To Jared Filega," said her mother.

Rosemarie scrubbed her reddened eyes.

"He—he said I just wanted to play at revolution, that all I knew were silly slogans. He said that was all very well in America, but I was wasting his time. He—he said he only invited me to come because he wanted to sleep with me."

She took a deep breath and launched into what Tracy realized was the final outrage perpetrated by Filega. "He compared me to you!"

She looked accusingly at her mother. "He said you were a real woman—n-not silly like me. He said you'd never have been fooled because you—you were sharp, that you listened and didn't talk all the time. And he said—he said you were better in bed."

Tracy cast her eyes demurely downward.

"That was when I hit him," Rosemarie said.

"And he hit you back?"

Rosemarie nodded, her voice thickening again with tears. "He knocked me down. Then he picked me up and knocked me down again. Then he threw me across the bed and I thought he was going to—to—but he didn't. He threw my suitcase at me and told me to g-get my ass out of his country. And he—he told me to give you his regards."

She put her head down on the table and howled. Tracy put her arm across her daughter's heaving shoulders and patted he back soothingly.

"I'm sorry, honey." Her voice was gentler, more familiar.

Rosemarie shook her head miserably. "He—does like you," she hiccuped.

"Jared was mean when he was young, and he's probably a lot worse now that he's got power," said Tracy. "But I'm sorry you had to find it out. How much did he hurt you?"

"Mostly my eye. And well—nobody had ever—"

"It's humiliating, isn't it? The important thing is you're home and it's over, Rosemarie."

"Did he—hit you?" Rosemarie asked.

"Not like that. He could get rough under—any circumstances."

Rosemarie nodded, and there crept into her face the first sign of affection Tracy had seen in two years. She put her arms around her mother's neck and buried her head against her. Tracy rocked her for a few minutes as she would have a five-year-old, then gently detached herself.

"Let's put some ice on that eye," she said, and couldn't understand why Rosemarie began to cry harder.

"I'm sorry, Mom," she wept. "I'm sorry."

After a while, they went upstairs and unpacked Rosemarie's bag.

"It's sort of nice to be back," said the new Rosemarie.

"It's nice to have you back," said her mother. "Not that there's much left to come back to."

"You still haven't told me—"

Tracy told her, briefly. She was so tired of the subject that she omitted how she had been saved from death by sling-back shoes.

Rosemarie listened with mounting horror. "Why are you writing this book if it's causing all this trouble?"

"I don't think I am, anymore."

The doorbell rang, and Tracy glanced nervously at her watch. "Oh, my God, that's my editor and my publisher and my ghostwriter. They wanted to come over and discuss things with me."

"To talk you out of it, I expect."

Tracy shook her head. "I haven't reached the point where I think I'd be better off dead, honey, and that's about where we are now. I never imagined this would happen. I still don't understand it. I haven't had an invitation to anything in weeks, and people seem to cross the street when they see me coming. I mean, all this over a social history?"

"Obviously, somebody thought it was going to be a lot more than a history. Maybe those items in *Spy* were the problem," Rosemarie suggested.

"I still don't understand. But I think I'd better forget about it. Which is too bad, because I could certainly use the money."

She patted Rosemarie's shoulder and was pleased to see that her daughter didn't pull away. Maybe she had something to be grateful to Jared for, after all, Tracy thought.

"Why don't you get some rest while I take care of this?"

Rosemarie nodded. She felt a good deal younger than seventeen, and she was content to leave whatever was going on to her mother, who suddenly seemed reliable and competent.

The doorbell rang again, insistently. Robert Mortimer was not accustomed to being kept waiting on suburban doorsteps. Tracy fluffed up her hair, straightened her blue sweater over her white silk pants, and scurried downstairs. She opened the front door as the doorbell jangled once more. Clustered on the steps were Mortimer, Kennally, Clayton, and a man Tracy had never seen before. The only things she noticed about him were his protuberant eyes and lack of chin. She hugged Clayton, who looked agitated, but he had been nervous since the burglary and had gone so far as to buy himself a gun, which Tracy had been dubious about.

"It's only for my—our—protection," he said.

"Do you know how to use a gun?" she asked. Clayton was the kind of investigative reporter who was most at home with files. He avoided physical confrontation and concentrated on being aggressive over the telephone. In moments of stress, he knitted—quite well, as far as Tracy could gather from a ski sweater he wore around the house. But she couldn't visualize him drawing down on anybody. He'd shown her the gun, a .22-caliber pistol.

"It's a small gun," he pointed out.

"But do you know how to use it?" she asked again. It didn't look as if it would be much use for beating an intruder over the head.

"I know how to fire and load it," said Clayton defensively.

Tracy grinned. "Not in that order, I hope."

She didn't think Clayton's gun was likely to constitute much of a defense against anything or anybody. She hoped he wouldn't shoot his foot off, especially since he insisted on keeping the weapon in the top drawer of his desk. She hoped she had successfully persuaded him not to carry it.

"Clayton, dear," she said. "So nice to see you."

Jerry Kennally embraced her in a more definitive manner. After a conversation with Clayton, Kennally had decided he might have to be more persuasive with Tracy than he had previously thought necessary. Not that he minded. She was an extraordinarily good-looking woman, and this was a case where duty would indeed be a pleasure. Although he had to admit she looked a little worse for wear. There were shadows under the wide blue eyes that hadn't been there the last time he saw her.

"We have to take good care of you," he told her warmly.

Tracy smiled wanly and held out her hand to Mortimer, who took it in both of his and bent his intense dark gaze on her. "Morty," she said, "nice to see you again."

Mortimer flinched slightly at the "Morty," but continued to smile.

"Tracy, dear. I want you to know we're behind you. All the way," he said.

She nodded and looked questioningly at the chinless factotum standing two paces behind Mortimer. The publisher gestured casually over his shoulder.

"This is Don Gargle. My executive assistant."

Gargle offered a weak smile and a limp handshake, then resumed his customary stance behind his employer. Gargle was a corporate gofer, and there was nothing executive about him. He had been a moderately successful political flack before he discovered he could make far more money by subjugating both his will and his pride to Robert Mortimer. If Mortimer approved of Tracy Gilmartin, Gargle approved of Tracy Gilmartin. If Mortimer lost interest in Tracy Gilmartin, she ceased to exist for Gargle. Kennally and Gargle detested each other, and Mortimer knew it and encouraged it. He employed Kennally because he was competent, though, and requisitely ruthless. He considered Gargle a corporate version of his butler. Mortimer didn't mind Kennally and Gargle's hostility toward each other because that meant he didn't have to worry about their getting together against him.

Tracy ushered them into the house and into the room that Tommy had used as a study, where there was a television set and a sectional tweed sofa on which they arranged themselves, with Mortimer flanked by Gargle and Kennally, and Clayton perched at the far end.

"I apologize for the state of the house," said Tracy with a wry smile.

Mortimer shook his head sympathetically. "Outrageous, outrageous." He gestured toward the television. "Did you see me on the late news the other night? I was interviewed on this disgraceful business."

He looked reproachfully at Gargle, whose hints to the networks that Mr. Mortimer was also available to offer his views on freedom of speech on the morning talk shows had been met with uninterest. Gargle looked sadly at his well-polished shoes.

Tracy shook her head. "I'm sorry, I didn't." She smiled, and even Mortimer was impressed by the way the smile lit up the room. "I've been sort of preoccupied with one thing and another. And the phone's rung constantly. This is the first day I've had anything like peace and quiet," she said.

Mortimer frowned. "Well, it's important we maintain your visibility, you know."

"Why?" she asked.

Clayton groaned inwardly. Kennally became attentive, and Gargle watched Mortimer, whose smile had congealed.

"I don't think I can go ahead with the book," said Tracy. "I mean, somebody's trying to kill me."

"All the more reason. There's a matter of principle involved now," Mortimer proclaimed.

"Absolutely," said Gargle.

"We can set up security for you. And get the house fixed," Kennally volunteered.

"You could move into my house. I have plenty of room," Clayton offered.

"It's not just that I'm scared, which I am," said Tracy. "I never dreamt this book would upset people the way it seems to have done. I don't understand it, and I've just about stopped trying to understand it."

Mortimer pursed his small mouth.

"Tracy," said Kennally, "I think Robert's right that you have to consider the question of principle. We can't allow these hired killers to shut you up! It's important that you be allowed to say what you have to say, write what you have to write. I mean, we consider this a very important book. And there *is* the question of money."

"I know," said Tracy, who had already banked a sizable check from Wissip Golight. "And I'll give it back. As soon as I can."

"There *is* a contract," said Gargle.

Tracy looked at him with distaste. "But if I give back the money, surely—"

"That isn't the point, Tracy, dear," said Mortimer glacially. "The point is we feel we—and you—must stick to our guns. To back down now would be to let them—whoever is doing this to you—win. We must stand up for our rights, and the First Amendment is one of our rights."

Gargle nodded emphatically, and Kennally wondered whether Mortimer planned to repeat all of his television script or only part of it. Tracy was looking miserable, but her lower lip was jutting in a manner Clayton had come to recognize as connoting stubbornness.

"I just don't think it's worth it," she said slowly. "When I started working with Clayton, it was fun and I enjoyed it. It's turned into—a—a nightmare. I just want to be left alone."

Her voice began to wobble.

Kennally reached over and took her hand in a strong, warm clasp. "Tracy, you're overwrought and upset, and no damned wonder," he said firmly. "I think we ought to move you into a hotel suite—or even to New York?"—he looked questioningly at Mortimer, who nodded affirmatively—"and let you relax and think about things for a few days.

You need rest. You need to know somebody's taking care of you."

He smiled at her in a manner that made clear who was going to be taking care of her. Twenty-four hours a day, if necessary. He was also going to have to work on Clayton, who was showing more sympathy for Tracy than Kennally felt was entirely necessary.

Tracy wavered. Kennally was the kind of man she liked, aware that she probably shouldn't. And it would be nice to let him take charge. Their eyes clung for a moment.

Mortimer, watching, smiled thinly. There was more than one reason he had hired Kennally. His dexterous handling of recalcitrant women writers was proving a distinct bonus. Not that Mortimer considered Tracy a writer. Tracy was a source to be mined, and the fact that she was photogenic, telegenic, and charming was useful. He had no interest in her himself. Mortimer had a long-standing rule that he did not allow his business to be interrupted by pleasure, especially sexual pleasure. He took more satisfaction in being invited to parties with prominent people present. He liked seeing his photograph in the social pages and his name on White House guest lists, although he hadn't managed that so far with President Sam Potter.

Mortimer recalled with evil glee what Kennally had told him of Potter's sexual proclivities as described by Tracy. But she had refused to follow through on it, in fact, had refused even to have it included in the outline. Mortimer's mouth became a button. He would have to give both Clapper and Kennally their marching orders on this, because his own prestige was involved in the publication of the Gilmartin manuscript. The Mortimer prestige was not to be trifled with.

"Then may we take it that you will allow us to—ah, look after you, Tracy?" Mortimer asked with an almost imperceptible glance at his watch. She hesitated. "I'd like to think about it, if you don't mind."

"Of course." He did mind, but that would give him time to make the situation crystal clear to Clapper and Kennally. Mortimer didn't doubt Tracy could be persuaded. He knew how badly she needed money, because she had confided her financial woes to Clayton, who had relayed them to Kennally. The size of the advance check had been tailored to make her eager for the rest of it. Mortimer was prepared to offer more, if necessary, in view of the free publicity the book had already received. Mortimer stood up, and Gargle rose simultaneously. Tracy seemed woebegone as they took their leave.

Kennally enfolded her in a close embrace. "I'll be in touch tomorrow and we'll set everything up to get you out of town," Kennally whispered, and kissed her gently on the cheek.

Tracy smiled at him. Her eyes were misting. She hated to be difficult with people who were trying to be nice to her.

More than that, they were offering her money she desperately needed. And poor Clayton was so obviously worried she wouldn't finish the manuscript. He looked frantic. Tracy hugged him. There were times when Clayton reminded her of a depressed bloodhound.

She went back to the kitchen when they had left, sat down at the table, and leaned her head on her hand. She supposed she ought to check on Rosemarie, but she was probably asleep. She'd looked as if she needed a week of it.

Tracy didn't feel like dealing with Rosemarie's problems. She didn't feel like coping with anyone's problems, including her own. Life presented a dismal picture at this point. She seemed to have the choice of rescuing herself financially by completing the book or having Clayton complete it, which was likely to get her killed. She couldn't sleep at night because she lived in dread of the next variation on the poisoned umbrella or the Clean Sweep bombers. And she couldn't call anybody for sympathy because practically none of her old friends seemed to be speaking to her, except members of the press who would now print anything she said. Even her pets were gone, not that she'd owned them for long, and she was afraid to replace them.

Tracy missed Benjamin and Chirp. They had been companionable, and their hatred of each other had kept her constantly alert to the possibility that Chirp would wind up in Benjamin's gullet. A tear trickled through her fingers onto the table. When the doorbell rang again, she jumped.

Perhaps if she ignored it, they'd go away, thinking she wasn't home. On the other hand, if they assumed she wasn't home, God knew what they'd do to the house this time.

Tracy heaved herself to her feet. She walked to the front door and didn't even peer through the little peephole at the side to identify the caller. Let them murder her! That way she'd get some sleep. She opened the door—and was swept off her feet, engulfed in a fierce embrace.

"My darling! My love! You are safe! I am here!" announced Dim.

Chapter Fourteen

Dim hadn't really thought about Tracy until she left him. He was delighted to have her with him, on his yacht and in his bed. She was attractive, affectionate, appreciative, and entertaining, but all of that didn't make her much different from a number of women he had known.

It was the manner of her departure that got his attention. His first reaction was anger and disappointment. He tore up the note she left him, barely glancing at its contents. Then he noticed that she had left all the clothes he'd bought her neatly hanging in the closet of the yacht's master bedroom. That was unusual. Still furious, Dim retrieved the pieces of Tracy's letter from the wastebasket, taped them together, and studied her words. The letter puzzled him. She told him how wonderful he was and how fond of him she was. Then she announced she had to leave because she had decided what he really liked about her were her gossipy stories. He was more interested in her gossip than in making love to her, she told him candidly. But she thanked him very much and she was sorry she had to do this and she sent her love.

At first he was exasperated. Such nonsense! Then he

read the letter again and pondered. Perhaps he *had* treated her as nothing but a source of entertainment at a time when what she needed was his affection and reassurance. He could hardly complain about her requirements for such reassurance, flattering as they were to an ego still smarting from the amused scorn of Marcia. He was touched by her effort to explain her departure so that she would not hurt his feelings. And he was impressed by her refusal to accept the gifts he had bought her. That meant she had gone home in the red silk dress she had worn at the White House dinner two weeks earlier.

Dim found himself thinking about Tracy instead of calling one of the regiment of women listed under various categories in his Rolodex. Flipping through its pages, he found none of them interesting enough to make him pick up the telephone. Not even Silver Quest, the rock singer whose appetite for the earthy things in life exceeded that of Dim. Not Marcia, whose beauty was exceeded by her financial acumen; she liked to discuss stocks and bonds in bed.

Dim had moped on his yacht. He didn't even enjoy eating and drinking as much as usual. He went out to get drunk in a favorite Greek bar one night and came home not only before closing time, but without indulging in his favorite pastime of smashing most of the glasses, which were automatically put on his bill. The bartender, who knew him well, anxiously asked after his health.

Dim went back to his yacht and sat on deck, moodily sipping cognac and realizing how much he missed Tracy. He sat up all night thinking about her. And when he turned on his television set and discovered that Tracy was in trouble, he knew exactly what he was going to do. He leapt into his Lincoln and hurtled to her rescue.

He found Tracy's house easily because it was the only one on the street that looked as though it had been in an air raid. The garage door was pasted over with plywood, awaiting repair, the windows on one side of the house were boarded up, and the lawn was littered with glass and debris.

"My poor little darling," Dim cried, charging to the front door, while up and down Roxbury Street, curtains twitched as occupants watched avidly for the next installment of their local soap opera. What opened the door to his thunderous knock looked both poor and little. Tracy looked bewildered, pathetic, rumpled, and, in Dim's eyes, absolutely adorable. He couldn't remember a woman who needed him so much. He scooped her up in his arms and kissed her comprehensively.

"There is nothing to worry about anymore," he assured her between kisses. "*I* am here. I am here to take care of you. I am going to take you away and nobody will ever hurt you again."

He put her down briefly, the better to proclaim, "From now on, they deal with *me*, Dim! If they dare!"

"Dim," said Tracy breathlessly, "where did you come from?"

"I missed you. I was lonely," he said. "I have decided I love you and we should be together. You want us to be together, do you not?"

"I—" said Tracy.

He shook his head. "No, no, don't worry. Your dear little letter was quite correct. I was wasting time making you tell me silly gossip when I should have been paying attention to you. Making love to you!"

He picked her up in his arms and headed joyously toward the stairs, where he was met by Rosemarie coming down to investigate the noise.

Dim paused, but did not put Tracy down.

"This is my daughter, Rosemarie," Tracy said weakly.

Dim set her down carefully and held out his hands to Rosemarie, who backed away slightly.

"Rosemarie! You are beautiful like your mother. I am

Dimitri Stavropoulos, and everyone calls me Dim. I am here to take care of your mother," he announced.

Rosemarie swallowed as her hands were engulfed in his large, sinewy paws. "I'm pleased to meet you, Mr.—"

"Dim! Dim! We shall be friends, Rosemarie, and you shall come and stay with us often!"

"Mother?" said Rosemarie plaintively.

Tracy clung to the banister. She tried to stem the flood. "Dim, could we stop just a minute—and talk?"

Dim looked at her worriedly and wrapped an arm around her waist. "Of course, my darling. We can talk about anything you care to. But I thought you didn't want to talk?"

"Just a little," said Tracy.

They went back downstairs and into the study. Tracy was beginning to feel as though her life were passing in processional between the study and the kitchen, punctuated by ominous creaks from the sitting room walls.

"Sit down, darling," said Dim protectively, and sat her down on the sofa, his arm firmly around her. Rosemarie looked pale, Tracy noticed, her bruised eye a dramatic splash of charcoal gray and red against the whiteness of her face. She also noticed that Rosemarie apparently had bathed and put on a clean pair of jeans and a pale blue sweater she had spurned when Tracy gave it to her as a Christmas present. With her blond hair streaming over her shoulders, she looked like a battered Alice in Wonderland.

"Dim," Tracy began, "I don't quite understand—"

Dim stroked her face tenderly. "It is very simple. You left and I came to bring you back. You do want to come back."

It was more of a statement than a question.

"I'm a little confused," she admitted.

He nodded. "That is why you need me. You need to be taken care of. You need to be taken somewhere warm and beautiful where you are safe and these terrible things cannot happen to you."

He uttered a harsh sound and clutched Tracy to him. "They might have killed you and I would never have found you again!"

Tracy decided it was comforting to know somebody cared whether she was dead or alive, without also being concerned about a literary publication date. She moved a little to free herself, mostly because her ribs were in danger of being crushed.

An expression of anguish crossed Dim's dark, craggy face. "I have upset you, Tracy, darling? What have I done? I came as fast as I could. I know I should have been here sooner, but I was a fool. I didn't realize for two whole weeks that I could not live without you!"

He picked up her hand and kissed each finger. Rosemarie watched the scene with a puzzled expression.

"Dim. Dim, dear," said Tracy with an attempt at firmness. "I'm not upset with you. I—I think it's wonderful that you're here. And I'm very glad to see you."

She realized suddenly that she was telling the truth. She *was* very glad to see him. She'd become very fond of him during their brief time together, and had she not been caught up in a maelstorm of inexplicable and violent events, she would have missed him a great deal more. There was a lot of the lovable bear about Dim. Tracy took a deep breath and tried to look objectively at her situation. Perhaps Dim was the answer. God knew, he could certainly take her away from it all. Anywhere she wanted to go. She looked at him and smiled the smile that had haunted his dreams.

His grin almost split his face, and he nestled her in his arms again. "Now it is all settled and we can be comfortable. Now we can talk," he said happily.

"Mother?" Rosemarie said again. Tracy smiled at her. "Mother," she repeated, "Who is Mr.—Mr. Dim?"

She sounded about six years old, Tracy thought, and remembered how fond she had been of Rosemarie when she was six years old.

Dim suddenly removed one arm from around Tracy and stretched out his hand to Rosemarie. "We shall be great friends," he said enthusiastically. "You are the daughter I have always wanted!"

Rosemarie looked startled, then pleased. Tracy began to laugh helplessly.

"Poor Rosemarie," she said. "It's all right, really. This is my—my dear friend Dim. And I guess maybe he *is* going to look after us."

"No maybe about it," Dim boomed. "We will leave tonight! Now!"

"Me too?" Rosemarie asked doubtfully.

"You can lie in the sun on my yacht, " said Dim. "Tracy and I, we are going to my island in the Aegean."

"You own an island?" Rosemarie asked.

"My family's island," said Dim. "It is beautiful. Quiet. Nobody will disturb us there. We will make love and talk—but not too much talk. Tracy is tired of talking. But if you want to write a book, my darling, you shall write it. You will do anything you want to and nobody will try to stop you! All right?"

"All right," Tracy agreed, leaning against his shoulder, which felt comfortable, familiar and as solid as a rock. Now that Dim had reappeared and established himself as a staple ingredient of her life, her normal spirits were beginning to rise. She'd been crushed and cowed by what had happened to her, but she'd been alone then, because Clayton didn't count as support in a situation where he felt equally imperiled. And Wissip Golight cared only about keeping her alive past her book's publication date. But now she had Dim. Perhaps he was right. Why shouldn't she finish the book? Then sail off into a Greek sunset and leave it all behind her. She looked at him with eyes that melted his heart.

"You really mean it?" she asked.

He held her close. "How can you ask? I have thought and

thought for days. Weeks. I know what I want. I want you. I want you with me always. I will—I will even marry you, Tracy! You must never leave me again!"

He kissed her. When she surfaced, Tracy mentioned breathlessly that she was still married.

Dim brushed it off. "No matter. A legality. Your husband—your former husband, I should say—he is in Canada, is that right? With a *man*?" His voice dripped scorn and Tracy looked nervously at Rosemarie, but her daughter did not appear to feel called upon to defend her father. She was staring at Dim with fascination.

"That's right," said Tracy.

"Then my lawyers will contact him," said Dim, and dismissed the Tommy factor.

"Mother," said Rosemarie, "are you going to marry Mr.—I mean Dim?"

Tracy relaxed against Dim's beautifully tailored shoulder. "Can you think of any reason why not?" she asked, and Dim uttered a fond, rumbling sound.

Rosemarie shook her head. The idea of life on a Greek island was blurring her desire for revolutionary martyrdom, especially in the squalor that Jared preferred.

"I think it's a great idea," she said.

Tracy held out her hand and Rosemarie found herself snug within the embrace of both her mother and Dim. To her surprise, she was enjoying it. "What about your book?" she asked.

Tracy looked thoughtful. "What do you think, darling?" she asked Dim. She shrugged.

"Write it, if it amuses you. Believe me, you will be perfectly safe, because now you have me!"

"Mmmm," said Tracy. "Maybe I will finish it," she reflected. "I could bring Clayton to your island, couldn't I?"

"Clayton?" Dim asked with a frown.

"My ghostwriter. I talk and he writes it."

Dim's brow cleared. "Ah. Of course. But not at once. We

want to be alone for a while, my little love. Just you and me. Then Clayton can come over in my plane. But not for too long. I want you to myself."

Tracy sighed contentedly. "I'd better call Clayton and tell him, because he's sick with worry that I won't finish it."

"Without me," said Dim firmly, "you would not have finished it."

Reluctantly he let her leave his arms to go to the telephone, and directed his attention to Rosemarie. "Your eye? You hurt it."

"Sort of. Somebody—somebody hit me."

Dim snarled softly. "Who? Where is he? Who?"

Rosemarie regarded him with growing affection. "He doesn't matter anymore," she said truthfully.

Dim was still clenching his fists. He'd been angry with a lot of women, but he despised a man who would hit a woman. "You are Tracy's daughter," he said. "Anyone who hurts you deals with me."

Rosemarie beamed at him.

Clayton was overjoyed by Tracy's news. Not only was the manuscript to be finished, but it was to be completed on a private Greek island under the protection of a multimillionaire whom Tracy all of a sudden was marrying. He couldn't believe his luck. He hadn't shared Kennally's confidence that Tracy would be persuaded to resume work on the book, given not only her doubts about it, but her fear of being murdered. And the manuscript still had a lot of gaps. He had a working draft, but it was far from complete, and there was the question of continuing friction over what Kennally wanted in and Tracy wanted left out, and Clayton was caught in the middle. Clayton suspected Kennally might be less suavely confident when confronted with the towering Greek.

"I can't believe it. When did all this happen?" he asked Tracy, who seemed to be her old bubbly self.

"Well, Dim arrived suddenly—and he sort of—took over." She blew a kiss to the Greek, who smiled fondly at her.

"And you're going to his island when?" Clayton could hardly wait for his personal invitation.

"Well, it's up to Dim," said Tracy. "But I think he wants to get away as soon as possible. He says he's worried about me," she added cheerfully.

"He's right," said Clayton. "And I couldn't be happier for you, Tracy. What a great idea, working on his island. Just let me know when you want to get started."

"Dim says he'll bring you over. He has a plane."

Clayton's face was pink with happiness. A day that had begun in gloom was turning out to be the best in months.

"I have to go now," said Tracy. "But I'll be in touch soon. I'll try to finish another tape for you, mail it or drop it off or something before we leave."

"Wonderful. I'll be waiting to hear from you," said Clayton. He hung up and did a little hop around the room. With Stavropoulos behind them, he and Tracy could thumb their noses at the Washington establishment and she could write whatever she felt like.

Clayton thought of calling Kennally, then decided to let Tracy break the news. Kennally was a good guy, but Clayton found him a little too arrogant in that peculiarly English way that permitted unassailable self-confidence. Kennally despised Mortimer, but had no qualms about working for him. Clayton didn't think he could work for a Mortimer, but it had occurred to him that at some point in the future, it might be worthwhile investigating how the Mortimer millions had been acquired.

There had been rumors about Mortimer's gyrations with the stock market, and Clayton thought they bore watching and probing. Maybe he could put that together on Stavropoulos's island, too.

Clayton grinned broadly, and wandered into his kitchen

to fix himself a celebratory scotch and water. With the glass in his hand, he sat down at his computer and scrolled through some of the work he'd done on Tracy's book. It was an intriguing pastiche of gossip, observation, and anecdote that offered an unconsciously hilarious view of how business was done in the nation's capital, with some wonderfully broad-stroke word portraits of political and social luminaries. Some of it was funny, some would raise eyebrows, some was mildly shocking, but all of it was a nice juicy read for those who suspected the sons of bitches in Washington couldn't be trusted.

Clayton checked the records of his tapes and hoped Tracy would remember to mail him another tape before she left. He was grateful that he had had the foresight to keep all the tapes in a bank deposit box. He was still nervous about having any of them in the house.

Clayton sipped his drink and wondered about the whirlwind romance between Tracy and Stavropoulos. He and Tracy had apparently hit it off far beyond the hopes of those who had set Dim up to take Tracy's mind off literary pursuits. This would be one in the eye for them, Clayton thought with cheerful malice, especially those who'd taken out a contract on her. That was something he'd like to investigate, too, once he was sure he wasn't one of the targets. He hoped Dim would get her out of town as soon as possible. Clayton had grown very fond of Tracy, although he wouldn't have wanted to live with her.

He stretched and wandered into the kitchen to make himself some dinner. He thought of going out for a few beers and decided against it. He was tired from sheer relief. After eating, he went back to his office to tidy his desk and play back the last tape Tracy had completed. He'd been sleeping with it under his pillow since the bombing. The tape, and his gun. As he slipped the tape into the recorder, he started at a sound from the terrace. The glass door now had a new lock and double bolt system that wasn't in place at the moment because it was mild and he'd been sitting out there earlier in the day.

Clayton tensed and listened. He wasn't imagining it. Somebody was on the terrace, moving in the darkness. He reached stealthily for the gun in his desk drawer and drew it out, thankful that the room was dim, lit only by a lamp in the corner. He was surrounded by shadow. He turned slowly toward the door, clutching the gun, wishing he could remember more about how to use it. All he could think of was the splay-footed stance he had seen in police movies, but he seemed to be frozen in place. He heard the lock click, and his mouth turned dry. He leaned against the wall and raised the gun, clutching it with both shaking hands.

"Stop, or shi'll oot!" Clayton croaked. He didn't recognize his own voice. The door began to open and he saw an outline blurred behind the heavy beveled glass. The door creaked, and the shadow grew larger and more menacing in the gloom. Clayton closed his eyes and pressed the trigger, cringing at the explosion that followed.

When he opened his eyes, he saw he had shot Tracy.

Chapter Fifteen

The discovery that Tracy wasn't dead was all that kept Dim from killing Clayton. While Rosemarie wept over the crumpled figure with blood streaking its blond curls, Dim seized Clayton by the throat, which turned his face purple and prevented him from trying to explain what had happened. Not that Dim cared to hear any explanation. As far as he was concerned, his darling Tracy had been murdered, and he concluded that Clayton had been behind the previous attempts on her life. He passed on that conclusion, at the top of his magnificent voice, to the police who arrived with the ambulance, providing them with a new theory in the mystery of who was trying to kill Tracy Gilmartin.

The police persuaded Dim to let go of Clayton's throat, for which Clayton was grateful, as it not only allowed him to attempt to defend himself, but gave him some solid blue-uniformed bodies as a buffer between himself and the Greek. He was even more grateful to the paramedics who examined Tracy and pronounced her alive.

They all went to the hospital, and Tracy was rushed into surgery. What looked like the makings of a medium-sized convention gathered. The press arrived in a swarm, bearing cameras, microphones, tape recorders, and even ballpoint pens. Clayton held—reluctantly—a press conference, occasionally interrupted by murderous threats from Dim. He tried to explain the terrible accident, pointing out that he had every reason in the world to keep Tracy alive.

"All I could see was what looked like somebody coming in my terrace door. And I'd already been burgled," he said.

"But you said they used a key." a reporter shouted.

"That didn't mean anything!" Clayton cried. "These were maybe the same people who've been after Tracy—they'd have got a duplicate! I mean, they've been dropping bombs and firing poisoned darts. Anyway, it isn't difficult to pick a lock, especially if you're a professional."

"You had no reason to think Mrs. Gilmartin was coming to your house?" another questioner asked.

"None at all. I thought she was on her way to the Aegean with Mr. Stavropoulos and her daughter. I'd talked to her on the phone a few hours earlier. I was going to join her there, to finish the book we were working on. Everything was fine!"

Clayton almost cried when he thought about how fine everything had been. He was uncomfortably aware of Dim's basilisk glare; he didn't doubt the Greek would try to carry out the threat he had made when he came rushing from his car to find Tracy lying on the floor, still clutching the tape she'd planned to drop off at Clayton's house, Clayton still clutching a gun.

"If my Tracy is dead, I will kill you," Dim had promised, in a voice more menacing because it was low-pitched. Clayton shuddered at the recollection.

"I didn't even aim," he said brokenly. "I don't know anything about guns. I'd never fired a gun before. I only bought it to scare them off—those people who kept robbing my house. I just closed my eyes and pressed the trigger. How could I have known *who* it was. I couldn't even see them."

"All the more reason to wait," said the cold voice of Dim.

Clayton looked at Rosemarie, who was sobbing on Dim's shoulder. "Rosemarie, you know I wouldn't hurt your mother. We were close friends."

"I'll never forgive you!" Rosemarie wept. "Never!"

Dim patted her gently.

"I'll never forgive myself," Clayton said miserably, and paled as a green-clad surgeon appeared in the doorway. Dim and Rosemarie rushed to the doctor, and Clayton stood waiting. It seemed to him that several years passed before Dim and Rosemarie returned to the waiting room. He took faint comfort from the fact that Dim did not immediately attack him.

"H-how is she?" he asked in a trembling voice.

According to Tracy's doctors, her condition was more of a fluke than a miracle. The bullet had merely grazed the top of her head, possibly because of Clayton's clumsy aim. Not only was she alive, but her condition was stable. There seemed, they said, no reason why she shouldn't make a good recovery. She was still unconscious, but her vital signs were satisfactory. She had, said the surgeon, been very lucky.

"So have you," said Dim, looking directly at Clayton, who had collapsed into a chair, feeling as though he were about to throw up. The press drifted away to file their stories, defanged by Tracy's insistence on living. Only Dim, Rosemarie, and Clayton remained.

None of them wanted to leave, despite the doctor's insistence that Tracy might remain unconscious for some time. Dim sat on a sofa, his arm around Rosemarie, whose sobs had become a snuffle, and Clayton cringed on a straight-back chair in a corner. Clayton was dozing when a nurse touched his arm and said he had an urgent telephone call from a Mr. Kennally in New York. He saw Dim's black eyes become suspicious slits.

"Kennally is Tracy's editor," Clayton explained. "He must have heard on the news about what—what happened."

"That damned book," said Dim.

"What in the name of God is going on?" asked Kennally. He had been roused from sleep by Robert Mortimer asking why Tracy Gilmartin's ghostwriter had tried to kill her.

Clayton told his story again.

"Jesus Christ," said Kennally. "I can't believe this. You mean you didn't even know what you were shooting at, old boy? You're a dangerous kind of fellow to have around the house, aren't you?"

"It's been a difficult time," Clayton said with careful control. He didn't want to antagonize Kennally.

"But she's all right? That's the main thing. How long will she be in the hospital?"

The unspoken question, thought Clayton, was how soon would she get back to work on the book. He was beginning to think publishers were even more venal than politicians.

"She's still unconscious," he pointed out. "We won't know how she is or how she's feeling until she wakes up."

"What's all this about the Greek?" Kennally asked.

Clayton told him.

"So she's going to finish the manuscript on his island? I must say, little Tracy has done rather well for herself," Kennally observed, thinking wistfully that he would never be required to offer Tracy twenty-four-hour-a-day protection.

"Well, I assume she's going to finish it," Clayton said nervously.

"What do you mean, you assume so?" Kennally's voice sharpened. Mortimer didn't like to hear news of failure, and he was inclined to take it out on the bearer of bad tidings, which in this case was apt to be Kennally.

"I just don't know," Clayton said harshly. "For God's sake, she's been shot. She hasn't even regained consciousness. She's lucky she isn't dead. And all you can think about is that goddamned manuscript."

Kennally became placating. "Sorry, old boy. I didn't mean to sound callous. Christ, I'm just horrified at the whole thing. Shocked! Mortimer is, too. All we want is for Tracy to get well, of course. Anything we can do to help—special doctors, anything at all. Just ask. We've already sent flowers."

Clayton listened and closed his eyes. He knew what Kennally was saying and why he had called and Kennally knew he knew. Kennally also knew Clayton had to play along. Clayton was in the unenviable position of being not only the man who had shot Tracy, but the man who was writing a book that already had triggered three assassination attempts.

"Clayton," Kennally said soothingly, "you ought to get some rest."

"I'd rest better if I knew I wasn't about to be charged with manslaughter," Clayton said bleakly.

"The grand jury won't indict, for God's sake. It was obviously an accident. Hell, you're the last person on earth who'd want to shoot her."

"I hope everybody agrees with you," Clayton said grimly. "I don't have any idea what she's going to say when she does wake up."

What Tracy did say when she woke up was nothing. She looked around her in bewilderment, at the mass of flowers ranged around the room, at the concerned faces looking down at her.

"My darling!" said Dim, hovering over her protectively.

Tracy smiled at him charmingly but distantly.

"Hello," she said.

The doctors moved in with a string of medical inquiries. Tracy smiled at them, too, touching the bandages around her head where her blond hair had been clipped away.

"I have a headache,"she said.

The doctors assured her that wasn't surprising.

Tracy looked with a puzzled expression at Dim and then at Rosemarie, who was holding her hand.

"Mother, are you really all right?" she asked anxiously.

Tracy's expression became bemused. She hesitated. "I—I'm your mother?" she asked.

Rosemarie burst into tears.

Dim looked at Tracy with alarm. "Tracy?" he said. "Do you know me?"

"Not really," said Tracy apologetically.

"Not really!" Dim wailed.

"Well," said Tracy with some of her previous tact. "You do look sort of familiar."

"We were going to be married!"

"Oh, dear," said Tracy.

"I'm your daughter!" cried Rosemarie.

"How—how nice," said Tracy.

"Amnesia," said the doctor.

When Dim and Rosemarie emerged from Tracy's room, Clayton, still ensconced in his chair in the corner, thought she might have died after all.

"My God, what is it?" he asked urgently.

Rosemarie looked at him angrily. "She's lost her memory," she said.

"She doesn't remember me," said Dim.

Clayton stared at them, and his relief became mixed with a nasty foreboding. "She can't remember *anything*?" he inquired slowly.

Rosemarie shook her head. "She can't remember her own name."

"Oh, my *God*," said Clayton.

He was overcome by the thought of having to tell Kennally and Mortimer that although Tracy Gilmartin was recovering, she could remember nothing. Which meant she couldn't finish her book, nor even confirm what had already been written. Which meant Clayton was out of work as a ghostwriter. His head swam. He sagged back in his chair.

Rosemarie looked at him with some compassion. "She *is* all right," she assured him. "The doctors say she was fantastically lucky. She'll probably be released from the hospital in a few days."

When Rosemarie smiled, she looked surprisingly like her mother. "She'll recover her memory, most likely," she said.

"She will?" Clayton seized on this glimmer of hope.

"Well, nobody knows when. But the doctors say it's possible."

"My little Tracy," said Dim in heartbroken tones. "She does not know me. She doesn't remember we love each other!"

Rosemarie patted his arm consolingly. "She will. And you can get to know each other all over again,"she suggested.

Dim brightened. "That's true! I shall woo her all over again! I wonder if she will be strong enough to travel? Of course, you would come, too, Rosemarie, to help look after her until she is well—"

"Of course," said Rosemarie happily.

Clayton risked a question. "What about—about her book?"

Dim looked thunderous. "No! No book!"

Rosemarie looked reproachfully at Clayton. "How can you think about that silly book now?"

The silly book was all Clayton *could* think about, now that he was assured of Tracy's recovery. "But if she did—recover her memory, she might want to finish it. I mean, she was so enthusiastic last—" His voice trailed away as a rumbling sound came from Dim.

"You mean before you tried to kill her, you—" He uttered what Clayton assumed was an expletive in Greek. "If she hadn't been thinking of that book, if she hadn't wanted to go to your house with the tape—to help *you*!—she would not be lying there now, my poor little darling, not knowing who she is, not knowing who *I* am!"

His voice rose, and Clayton backed away as a nurse rustled starched disapproval through the door of the waiting room.

"You people must keep your voices down. This is a hospital. People are sick," she informed them icily.

"We are very sorry," Dim said apologetically as he took Rosemarie by the arm.

"Come," he said. "You must have some rest. Then you will help me buy things for Tracy. Travel things. Island clothes. And for you, too!"

Rosemarie's eyes brightened. They walked past Clayton and headed for Dim's waiting limousine. Clayton felt the nurse's curious gaze.

"You look like you could use some sleep," she observed.

Clayton nodded. "I suppose so."

The nurse hesitated. "Your friend—Mrs. Gilmartin—is doing quite well. You might like to know that. She's chattering away."

Clayton looked at her hopefully. "Do you think I—could I possibly see her just for a moment? The accident was all my fault and I feel so terrible about it. I'd be so grateful if I could just—see that she really is alive."

The nurse considered. "Let me check with her doctor. I don't see why not, as long as you don't excite her. And you never know, you might jog something in her memory."

Clayton breathed a prayer as he watched her crisp back receding down a corridor. In a few moments, she returned.

"Just for a few minutes, now. I told the doctor you were so worried about her."

Clayton looked at her gratefully.

Tracy was sitting up in bed, chatting with a nurse about the flowers that had arrived. "The roses are lovely. Who did you say they were from?"

She read the card that was handed to her. "Robert Mortimer?" Her brow wrinkled. "Oh, dear, I wonder who that is. This is so annoying!"

She looked up as Clayton entered the room, and smiled, but there was no recognition in her eyes.

"Five minutes and no longer, Mr. Clapper," said the nurse.

"Tracy," said Clayton softly. "How are you feeling?"

"Just a headache is all." She uttered her familiar rippling giggle and Clayton's heart ached. "I just can't remember anything. I mean, I don't know who Tracy is. Or where I live, or anything. I didn't even recognize—what did he say his name was?—Dim, and I'm apparently supposed to marry him!"

Her eyes twinkled. "It's sort of funny, in a way. Like being reborn. But I feel bad because it upsets people that I don't recognize them. Even that pretty blond girl—my daughter, and I don't know her." She sighed.

Clayton hesitated. "You don't remember anything about—about a book, either?"

"A book?"

"You were writing a book. With me."

"I *was*? How exciting! What was it about?"

"Your life in Washington," said Clayton. "The people you knew, the parties you went to. You went to parties at the White House, Tracy. You know the President and First Lady. You know all kinds of people."

"Why was I writing about them?" She looked puzzled.

"Well, it was—sort of a social history. You were writing about what you knew about people. Politics. Funny things at social events. Things behind the scenes."

"I was writing a book about that kind of thing?" Her Mormon mother suddenly looked out of Tracy's face. She shook her head slowly, carefully, gently touching the bandages over which trendils of pale hair curled. "Those people were—are my friends? And I was writing things about them?"

"Is something coming back to you, Tracy?" Clayton's eyes searched the pale face, and he reached automatically for his notebook.

"You mean I was writing a gossip book," Tracy said severely.

"Sort of. Not really. Not quite." He began to back off, but it was too late. The new Tracy bent a gaze of disapproval on him.

"What a dreadful thing to do!" she said.

Chapter Sixteen

"Why are people sending flowers?" Jayne Millspaw asked. "It's so hypocritical. They're all sorry Clapper couldn't shoot straight."

The First Lady sighed. "Sam's very edgy about it all."

Jayne scratched at a speck on her pleated silk skirt. "No wonder we couldn't win in Vietnam," she observed tartly. "I mean, how could they manage to kill a cat and a canary and miss Tracy?"

"I don't know anything about that," said Linda Potter primly. "And of course Sam and I sent flowers."

Jayne sniffed. "Come on, Linda. There haven't been as many botched attempts to get rid of somebody since the last time the press buried Nixon. I hope somebody's testing the flowers before she smells them."

"Jayne," said Linda, "I really think this is—is tasteless. Tracy was our friend and she's still in the hospital and we should remember that. Anyway, nobody knows whether—"

"She'll get her memory back? They say she probably will. The bullet apparently hit her least vulnerable part, since it just nicked her head. What then, my dear?"

There was a short silence.

"You have to remember." Linda Potter went on, "She's gone through a dreadful experience. Several dreadful experiences, in fact. Why would she want to go on with that book that caused it all?"

"That may not be entirely up to Tracy. She has a publisher. And while I suppose he could get his money back, from what I know of Mortimer, he'd be more interested in staying in the middle of a juicy scandal."

Jayne Millspaw was right. Robert Mortimer sent his own specialists to the hospital to assess the likelihood that Tracy would live up to her financial potential. Mortimer considered her shooting a setback and her amnesia a complication. He was prepared to do anything for Tracy—or to Tracy—to restore her memory.

"Keep Clapper at her bedside twenty-four hours a day, if that'll help. Play tapes back to her. Run more neurological tests. Whatever it takes," he told Jerry Kennally.

"A frontal lobotomy?" Kennally murmured wickedly.

"Don't be silly," snapped Mortimer, "I want results."

Mortimer's instructions were unnecessary as far as Clayton was concerned. He was at the hospital every day, and so far he hadn't repeated Tracy's renunciation of gossip to Kennally. The trouble was that the only times Tracy wasn't smiling and cheerful were when Clayton told her some of the funny stories that she had related with such relish in the old days.

"So unkind," she would say, "Those nice people who sent me those beautiful flowers."

"They tried to kill you," Clayton protested.

Tracy shook her head. "I don't know that. You're the only one who tried to shoot me, but I don't hold it against *you*."

The only glimmer of hope appeared the day Tommy Gilmartin appeared unexpectedly at the hospital to identify himself as Tracy's husband and presumably alleviate belated feelings of guilt.

Tracy greeted him politely, but coolly. "He makes me

think of black suede," she told Clayton and Dim. She couldn't imagine being married to him, she added.

"That's probably because I'm comparing him to you, darling," she told Dim, who was rapidly re-establishing himself in her affections, if not in her memory. He enveloped her in a grateful embrace.

Clayton rushed to report to Kennally that Tracy had at least remembered something.

"He reminded her of black *suede*?" said Kennally.

"He reminded her of *something*. That's what counts. Maybe it's a breakthrough. God knows I could use one."

"Don't complain to me. If you listened to Mortimer, you'd think *I* shot her," Kennally said tiredly. Clayton sighed so heavily Kennally took pity on him. "Look, just hang in there. The doctors all seem to think it's just a matter of time. Once she starts remembering, she'll remember all the money she was going to make."

"She doesn't need money now. She's got Dim."

"Even so. It's nice to have your own. What if Dim walked out on her like her husband? She's been burnt once, don't forget."

"I wish I could think of something to help," said Clayton.

"You did get rid of that gun, didn't you?"

Clayton winced. "The police have it. I never want to see it again. I mean, I never owned a gun on my life before—"

"I believe you," said Kennally.

It would have surprised Clayton to know that Dim was as eager as he for Tracy to regain her memory, for quite different reasons.

Since the accident, Tracy had become almost bovine in her placidity. She liked to concentrate only on pleasant things, like the gifts Dim brought her daily and the charming stories Rosemarie told about when she was a little girl and Tracy was her mommy. Tracy felt as though she were floating. Rosemarie seemed to be as nice a daughter as anyone could want. She was attentive, affectionate, and solicitous, and she never mentioned Jared Filega or anything that might damage her image as a dutiful daughter. Rosemarie had come home to capitalism. She was disillusioned with her revolutionary phase, especially since the bruises inflicted by Jared had taken a long time to heal. And she was adjusting happily to living in the palatial apartment Dim had rented for the duration of Tracy's illness. She was not about to risk losing Dim's generous paternalism by giving voice to her worries about the wretched of the earth who had left her with little more than a black eye. Rosemarie had a lot invested in making sure her mother married Dim.

But Dim missed the old Tracy, who had been funny, provocative, and suprisingly shrewd and had told the best stories he'd ever heard. The new Tracy was very appealing, but her smile was as blank as it was bright, and her conversation tended to consist of cooing with delight at presents. Dim liked women to be intriguing, and while Tracy was as physically delectable as ever, she wasn't as psychologically titillating. Dim knew from past experience his growing restlessness in her presence was a herald of the kind of boredom he could afford to avoid. He also couldn't make love to a woman in a hospital bed.

When the doctors said Tracy could go home, Dim's exuberance returned. Once she was back with him, he told himself, she would start remembering things, and everything would be wonderful again. The largest limousine Rosemarie had ever seen was waiting at the hospital door for Tracy. It was equipped with a mink blanket, and champagne and a chauffeur who had been warned it would cost his job to jiggle the passenger. Behind the limousine was Clayton's Toyota. Clayton had not been invited to accompany Tracy on the ride home. Dim had decided Clayton probably hadn't meant to shoot Tracy, so that meant he was an incompetent fool.

"My darling is comfortable?" Dim inquired of Tracy, who

was almost invisible between the fur rug and his protective arm. His darling sipped at her champagne and sat up, pushing away the mink blanket. Dim looked at her in surprise.

"If you don't mind," said Tracy, "I'd like to go home."

"But we are going home."

"I mean to where I used to live."

"Roxbury Street?" said Rosemarie in tones of horror. "But it's still a mess, Mother. You don't even remember it, anyway. And you'll love Dim's apartment."

"I'm sure I shall," said her mother. "But I want to go to Roxbury Street first."

"Whatever you want, darling," said Dim. "But I don't understand. I mean, after what happened there—"

"That's the point," said Tracy. "I don't remember what happened there. And I'd like to."

"Why don't you have a nice rest at Dim's place and then we'll think about going to Roxbury Street tomorrow?" Rosemarie suggested.

"I don't need a nice rest. I've done nothing but rest for what seems like years. I'm bored."

Dim grinned, and told the chauffeur to change direction. The driver almost crushed Clayton's Toyota. Cursing, Clayton made an illegal U-turn to catch up with the limousine as it disappeared down a side street.

The house on Roxbury Street was a mess. It had a mildewed, discarded look. The debris had been cleaned up, but that was as far as rehabilitation had gone. Tracy stood at the front door, her face thoughtful. She turned to Rosemarie.

"You have a key?"

Gloomily, Rosemarie opened the door. Tracy wrinkled her nose as she looked at the devastated sitting room and the untidy kitchen. She went up the stairs, hesitated, then turned to the door of her bedroom and opened it.

"Well?" Dim asked gently. She shook her head. "You did choose your own room."

"I did?"

Dim sighed, and watched as Tracy pawed through some clothes in a disinterested way and peered at a photograph of Rosemarie in a camouflage suit.

"Fancy dress, dear?" she asked. Rosemarie smiled wanly.

Downstairs, Clayton was hovering at the front door.

Tracy waved at him. "I'm trying to remember things."

"Wonderful."

Tracy stopped at the sitting room door and shook her head. "Something's got to be done about this. I mean, we can't leave the place like this. We can't sell it like this, for one thing." She looked reproachfully at Rosemarie, who looked guilty.

Tracy went into the room with its blackened, scarred walls and exposed concrete flooring. Abruptly, she stooped and picked up a small yellow feather. She frowned. There was a silence as she fingered the feather, which seemed charred around its edges.

"Poor little thing," said Tracy.

"Who?" Clayton asked weakly.

"Chirp," she said softly.

Clayton uttered a yelp, and Dim scowled at him. Tracy looked puzzled.

"Chirp, chirp. Poor little thing. It's a feather from a little bird, isn't it?"

"Chirp," said Clayton, ignoring Dim, "was the name of your canary. The one that got killed when they put a bomb down the chimney of this room, Tracy. Chirp!"

Tracy looked at Clayton and then back at the feather. "Poor little thing," she said in the tone of one who had just received sad news. Clayton leaned against the wall.

"I think we should go home now," said Dim.

"I keep thinking I should be looking for something else," said Tracy.

Clayton nodded vigorously.

"Benjamin," he said.

"Benjamin?" Tracy asked.

"Your cat."

"What happened to him?"

"A poison dart—when you were taking him to the vet."

"Poor little thing," said Tracy.

"We are going home now," said Dim, as he shepherded Tracy toward the front door, where the paint was blasted off. She moved slowly and reluctantly.

"What is it?" Dim asked.

She turned troubled eyes on him. "Could we drive around a bit? I keep feeling as though I'm about to turn a corner in a road and see something I know. I really do. It's the strangest feeling."

"Of course," said Dim.

Tracy gestured toward Clayton. "Let him come, too. He wants me to remember."

Dim's face clouded. "As you wish. But we *all* want you to remember, Tracy, believe me. We want you to remember and be happy again."

She smiled at him. "This will make me happy, darling."

She positively skipped to the limousine, with Clayton cantering behind.

They drove all over the neighborhood, through Georgetown, down Connecticut Avenue, past the Lincoln and Jefferson memorials. Tracy stared out of the window, her face tense, while Dim held her in the circle of his arms and made sure the blanket covered her knees. Nobody spoke. Finally Tracy sighed and her blond head drooped on her slender neck.

"Maybe we should—go home, after all," she said in a small, discouraged voice.

Dim patted her comfortingly. "Tomorrow we shall try again," he said.

As the limousine headed down Pennsylvania Avenue,

past the White House, Tracy glanced casually at the home of the President and began to laugh.

"Why in the world would the White House make me think of a hairbrush?" she said, and her giggle rippled around the car.

Clayton was tense but said nothing. Only Rosemarie was openly scornful. "How silly!" she said.

Tracy burst into laughter again. "It was silly! That was what Sam always said! He felt so silly, but he—but he—" Her voice trailed away and the blue eyes became immense. "My God," said Tracy, "so did Vladimir."

"Tracy?" said Dim.

"Tracy!" said Clayton, and saw familiar glee in Tracy's face. Her laughter was unstoppable. She laughed until tears rolled down her cheeks and Dim began to look worried.

"My darling," he said, "you remember something?"

"Do I!" said Tracy. "No wonder they wanted to kill me!"

Chapter Seventeen

Even people who'd been trying to kill Tracy relaxed when the word filtered down the Washington grapevine that although she occasionally had flashbacks of memory, she remained far from recovery and was in fragile physical condition. This was the gospel as laid down by Robert Mortimer, who was determined that Tracy would survive until the book was published. He forbade all interviews, put Kennally in charge of distributing an occasional somber health report about Tracy, and made it worthwhile for Clayton to extend his leave of absence and disappear from the capital scene while he completed Tracy's book.

Tracy was happily ensconced in Dim's penthouse while her dilapidated house was cleaned, repaired, and sold. She was never left alone; Dim was happy to be at her side twenty-four hours a day. When he had to be gone on business, his chauffeur, who looked a bit like Clint Eastwood, was left on guard. Dim was delighted to have his gregarious, gorgeous Tracy restored to him. Clayton was awash in relief and optimism about his bank balance. Rosemarie spent most of her time shopping—with Dim's blessing—for clothes to wear on his island paradise.

Yet Tracy was not the woman Clayton had shot. She looked the same, she giggled the same way, but the bullet that had more or less bounced off her head had hurt her feelings. She could understand her friends might be cross with her for writing about silly things they'd done in the past. Yet she thought they might have given her credit for knowing the difference between social indiscretion and the kind of nastiness that could ruin a career. She hadn't meant to be disloyal or unkind, she reflected, as she lolled in Dim's jumbo Jacuzzi, she'd simply been worried about money.

When she thought about how sympathetic and understanding she'd always been about people's troubles, it stirred uncharacteristic anger in her that nobody had cared about hers. They could have come and talked to her, told her what they were worried about, and she'd have understood. They didn't have to poison Benjamin or blow up Chirp or try to squash her on the garage door to get their message across. It made her wonder what kind of friends they'd ever been, especially when she thought of the expensive flowers and solicitous notes that had arrived at the hospital. Conscience bouquets. Tracy wriggled in the scented water. It made her feel hollow inside, because she was pretty sure she knew who had taken out contracts on her. Coming so soon after learning about Tommy and his boyfriend in black suede—not that *they'd* sent any flowers—it had done a lot to destroy her faith in people.

She didn't talk about her disillusionment. She mostly brooded about it in the bathtub, because the rest of the time she concentrated on Dim, the only person who'd never let her down. She was determined not to lose him the way she'd lost Tommy. Dim had rescued her, and she was prepared to reward him with a thousand and one nights of gossip to add spice to a lifetime of devotion. She'd already had to persuade him she ought to finish the book as an act of loyalty to Clayton, the old friend who'd listened to her when nobody else had, even if he wasn't much good with firearms.

"I will not lose you again, my darling," Dim told her, engulfing her in a hug worthy of a grizzly bear.

Tracy kissed him. "You aren't going to lose me. I just feel I should do this. It's like your having to finish a business deal because it wouldn't be right to walk out on your partners. You know?"

Dim knew. He understood and appreciated that kind of logic, especially as he was currently engaged in putting the final touches on an immensely lucrative and diplomatically delicate arrangement involving arms shipments to a nation with which the United States was unobtrusively trying to improve previously frigid relations.

He did not mention to Tracy his quiet conversations on that matter with President Potter, whom Dim had met recently at an exclusive gathering of very rich men. Sam Potter had inquired after Tracy's health and expressed gratitude to Dim for taking care of her. It was too bad her memory hadn't returned, said the President, his eyes watchful. Dim shook his head and agreed that it was, but meantime, what they were most worried about was that she regain her strength. New memories could be fashioned, perhaps better memories, he observed, and Tracy was about to begin a life as his wife, living on his island. The President said sincerely that that was wonderful and to let him know the wedding date so that that he and Linda could send an expression of their affection. Dim nodded. He watched with a small smile as the President loped off to report to the First Lady that Tracy was leaving town, with any luck, for good. Linda Potter's smile glowed across the room.

Dim didn't tell Tracy any of that. One reason they got along so well was they omitted from their communications anything either thought would be upsetting to the other. Yet Dim was a man who believed in an eye for an eye, and he hadn't forgiven the Washington power clique for trying to kill Tracy.

He didn't care what the damned book was about; he didn't approve of killing women. As far as he was concerned, Tracy could go ahead and finish it, and he'd make sure that anyone who tried to stop her regretted it. He'd suggested they leave immediately for the Aegean on the grounds that it would be safer, but Tracy had proved surprisingly obdurate about being in Washington when the book was published, or at least when Mortimer published it in condensed, prepublication form in a magazine he'd recently acquired for that purpose. Mortimer had got a lot of mileage out of Tracy, and he anticipated getting a lot more. Dim's neighborhood was peppered with Mortimer's security men, and Kennally knew it would cost him his job if anything happened to Tracy at this stage. He spent so much time checking on her, she complained mildly she couldn't get any work done.

Kennally was delighted with the book, especially since Tracy not only regained her memory but developed a flourishing resentment against those who had tried to get rid of her. Clayton had created from her recollections, diaries, and notes a skillful jigsaw, weaving together what Kennally called an ear-witness account of two decades of political and social shenanigans. He had used Tracy's information bank as a base from which to explore and build a case against at least two Presidents and a dozen of Capitol Hill's more prominent lawmakers and hired guns.

Tracy had provided the key, but it was Clayton who knew how to unlock the doors. The book was an expert guide through smoky political mirrors, tracking the silly and the sleazy, illuminating the way deals were cut in shadowy places.

It was as discerning as it was sensational. It offered a glimpse of giants and gnomes in the looking glass of Washington, and a lot of it was funny. It was stuff on which columnists could happily graze, but it was a map for those who could read it, hinting at past, present, and future deals. It also hinted carefully, judiciously, at what Tracy would never have condoned before, the personal habits of people in high places. She'd never know for sure, but she was quite certain her old friends Sam and Vladimir had a hand in some of those strange events. So let them feel silly, she told herself; that would be nothing compared to what they'd almost done to her, after she'd been so nice to them.

Mortimer and Kennally salivated as they read the increasingly candid revelations of the woman they'd once thought of as Bambi. Nice people, observed Mortimer sagely, were much more dangerous than nasty people because they'd developed such a head of virtuous steam by the time they decided to stop being sweet. Kennally agreed with him, although he assumed Mortimer had no personal acquaintance with niceness, merely a desire to exploit its potential.

Tracy was almost forgotten on the social scene where she had once been so ubiquitous. A few invitations came to Dim, but none was accepted, and gradually, as weeks grew into months, the name of Tracy Gilmartin faded in the memories of those who had known her. Only Eleanor McCluskey sometimes thought about her wistfully, but she never dared to call her. She hadn't even sent flowers when Tracy was shot, partly because she wanted to sever all connections with her and partly because she was terrified Uncle Francis would try again to kill the woman whom he viewed as a threat to his political connection.

It was, consequently, all the more of a shock when Mortimer's new magazine, renamed *Listen!*, hit the newsstands with a cover story about a new and stunning exposé of what was described as "down and dirty on D.C." The magazine carried a photograph of a beaming and obviously healthy Tracy, and an interview in which she asserted that what she had written had been known to "practically everybody" in Washington and she didn't see why other people shouldn't be aware of what went on behind the scenes.

Mortimer, in an editorial of vast rhetorical righteousness, managed to incorporate the phrase "the truth shall make you free" into a collection of platitudes about his long fight for the First Amendment, the fourth estate and the public's right to know. He portrayed Tracy as a latter-day Joan of Arc clinging to her concept of truth in the face of violence and evil. He had a good time writing it, and most people laughed at it, but there were few smiles in the White House or on Capitol Hill at the resuscitation, not only of Tracy, but of her book. The magazine sold out instantly, and was a topic of conversation in circles that would have surprised even Tracy.

President Potter had a long and solemn conversation with his reelection campaign managers, who were armed with Xerox copies of what they considered the most damaging references to his playing clandestine revolutionary games with Jared Filega and even more explosive games, politically speaking, in his bedroom.

"We did back off Filega," Potter pointed out.

"Depends on whether it was soon enough. It wasn't as if you weren't warned about that bastard," said Harry Butler, the campaign chief of staff. He'd spent a weary morning fielding press calls.

"What about the other stuff?" asked Press Secretary Jim Dibble, whose voice sounded as though it came from the depths of a tomb.

The President winced. He'd spent a miserable night discussing "the other stuff" with the First Lady. She had taken a pragmatic position: If he had to screw around, couldn't he be *normal* about it?

"I suppose it could have been worse. She could have said you were gay," Dibble said morosely.

"*I* don't think that would have been worse. At least he'd have got the gay vote," said Butler. "As it is . . ."

"What d'you want me to do? Not run again?" Potter asked harshly.

There was silence.

"It's hard to say," said the chief of staff at last. "For one thing, we don't know what else is coming. I mean, this was a condensation of the book."

"We can assume they used the best—I mean the worst—they had," said Dibble.

"Could we sue?" asked an assistant press secretary, and shrank before their stares of contempt.

"Can we ignore it?" asked the President.

"Maybe," said Butler. "Depends on the polls. Depends on public reaction. One thing, I don't think Congress is gong to call for a public investigation, because too many of them are involved."

"It *is* innuendo, a lot of it, but who's going to challenge her?" Dibble pointed out. "The best we can hope for is people will reject it as a bunch of nonsense from a bimbo. Except—"

"Except Clapper tied in a lot of solid stuff—Central America and assassination—that people have already heard of," said Butler.

"Charley Dill isn't running again. He told me this morning," said Potter.

"Jesus Christ," said Butler.

"The liberals practically beat him to death on the assassination stuff in the magazine," said Dibble.

"And that's what the far-right religious nuts—"

"Will do to me?" Potter finished the chief of staff's sentence.

The President slid lower in his chair, peering sadly around the Oval Office. "There has to be something," he said. Desperately, he searched the miserable faces surrounding him.

"Well, it's not as if anybody's left out," said Dibble thoughtfully. "I mean, she went after Winston Gusty as well. In terms of the campaign, it's so far along, we might just—well, throw ourselves on the mercy of the voters. Our polls have been great. The country's in good shape financially. People vote their pocketbooks, not their morals."

"What does the First Lady say?" Butler asked.

Potter sighed deeply. "She says she'll stand by me if I stay with the campaign for reelection. If I pull out, she says she'll divorce me. If you ask me, I think she'll divorce me anyway, in the end."

"Her hands aren't too clean, morally speaking," Dibble said bluntly.

Potter nodded. "But we both knew that. I mean, it's been pretty much a matter of convenience for a while now. But we kept up appearances. What she's maddest about is she thinks that—that other stuff makes her look silly."

"I'm not so concerned about that," Harry Butler volunteered. "It's so far out, a lot of people probably won't believe it. I think the real danger lies in the Filega connection and maybe in the assassination allegations. Except there's still a sizable percentage of the public that doesn't see much wrong with taking out a villain so we don't waste the lives of our American boys. And the Filega thing is complex. Maybe too much so for Joe Sixpack."

"You're optimistic?" Potter was incredulous.

"Hardly," said Butler. "But I don't think we should give up just yet. There was a hell of a lot of hype in that magazine piece."

"What about a press conference?" Dibble asked. Potter shuddered.

"You have to do that," said Butler. "No way around it. And I think you have to stonewall some, and deny the hairbrush business. That's her word against yours. I mean, they're not going to crucify you for a little extramarital scuffling around that happened before you got into the White House. Kink—that's something else."

"Remember Gary Hart," said Dibble.

"He wasn't President," said Butler, "and he managed to demonstrate a political death wish in the middle of a campaign. What we're dealing with is bad enough, but that isn't analogous."

"It may be worse," said Potter despairingly. "Maybe I should just pull out. I mean, how'm I going to get through a campaign with those buzzards in the press yelling about S and M?"

"I said we had to wait a bit. I'm not saying you won't have to pull out," said Butler.

"A lot," he added, "will depend on how you handle the news conference you've having tomorrow."

"Tomorrow?" Potter yelped.

The chief of staff nodded firmly. "That gives Dibble a chance to throw them some raw meat—the opportunity of having at you tomorrow, so he won't discuss it today. And we spend the rest of today figuring out your posture. Not to mention Linda's."

"Oh, God," said Potter. "I think I'd rather announce a pullout."

"That's an option," said Butler briskly, "that we have to consider, sir."

"What am I supposed to do?" Potter asked. "Go on national television announcing 'I am not a pervert'?"

Dibble smiled bleakly. "That's a variation of something that didn't work in Watergate, so maybe we should think of something else."

There was a quiet tap at the door of the Oval Office, and Dibble was called out. He returned a few minutes later, grim-faced.

"Senator Eleanor McClusky of Illinois is dead. She apparently took an overdose of sleeping pills last night."

The President stared at him. "But— Christ, she was

barely mentioned in the piece. Something trivial about her being more lonely then people realized. A reference to some party. I didn't read anything into that. Did you?" He turned to Butler, who pursed his lips.

"Maybe McClusky read something into it. Maybe she was afraid more was coming."

Again there was a long silence, broken by the chief of staff. "This could be a break," he said thoughtfully. "I mean, it's true that there seemed no more than a casual reference to McClusky. So this could be denounced as character assassination—or maybe we should use another word. But here is a woman who was considered an outstanding politician. Was she destroyed by vicious innuendo?"

Dibble brightened slightly. "That's a thought. Moreover," said Dibble, "Filega has strongly denied any dealings with the President of the United States beyond those on the public record. Now, we know what Filega is—or we do now—but as far as the public's concerned, he's been cleaning up his act a bit lately. Dismantled the death squads, for example. Talking about education."

Potter contemplated the presidential seal embossed on his desk pad. "By God," he said slowly, "maybe we do have a chance."

"It's still a maybe," said Butler. "But we've got more of a chance than poor McClusky. Whatever she did."

Chapter Eighteen

All Francis Sikorski knew was that his niece, his entrée to Washington, was dead, and it was Tracy Gilmartin's fault. He didn't care what Eleanor had done. He didn't even care why she'd killed herself. There was nothing in the *Listen!* article, as far as he could tell, that was so terrible. So there had been a little fast stepping in Washington, so what was new about that? Sounded to him like one of those confession pieces that whores wrote to get attention and make money. Why it should have upset Ellie so much, he couldn't fathom. She'd always seemed to him to be downright stuffy and self-righteous. Gave him the impression that she was looking down her nose at him sometimes, disapproving of him because of his life-style when he was simply making a buck like she was.

But he'd liked having even a snooty niece in the United States Senate. It had given him a certain clout with his peers in Chicago, and he'd always felt that someday it could be useful, because he knew Ellie was fond of her aunt and she wouldn't want anything to come out that would cast aspersions on the family name or her political future. He remembered how depressed she'd been about the clipping saying the Gilmartin woman was going to write a book, and he'd assumed it was because Gilmartin knew something Ellie was afraid she'd write about her.

That was why he'd decided to do Ellie a favor she hadn't asked for, and probably wouldn't, by dispatching old Benny to Washington to take care of things and let her stop worrying. Except Benny was more past it than Francis had realized. He'd never thought one of his old soldiers would botch something so simple. Not that any of the others had done any better, as far as Francis could tell from what he'd read about poisonings and bombings and dead cats. What a bunch of amateurs, he reflected sourly.

The only way to do a thing right was to do it yourself, and he felt he had to do something. It was a question of pride with him now. That Gilmartin broad had, in a manner of speaking, killed his niece, his only hope of political influence. Gilmartin had two strikes against her in his book and he intended to settle the score. Benny was useless; he'd been in a nursing home since he fractured his skull driving that car into Gilmartin's garage door, and was only semicoherent, which was probably just as well, under the circumstances.

Francis couldn't take any more chances this time. He had to pull in a professional, which would cost him, but he felt it was worth it, since it was, after all, a matter of family pride. He had an old friend who was an expert in explosives, who'd survived several hairy missions in the Middle East. Francis had never known him to fail, and anyway, setting up the operation would give him something to do other than mop up the tears of Ellie's aunt, who'd been crying ever since she heard the news. Francis believed in getting even.

Eleanor McClusky's death also upset Tracy, to the point that she almost refused to be interviewed on national talk shows about her book. Dim, who had read the manuscript with considerable amusement, tried to console her. "You said nothing, my darling, nothing about her. She must have been very depressed about something else."

Tracy knew she hadn't said anything incriminating about Eleanor, and she'd had no intention of doing so. She was fond of Eleanor, although she didn't share the senator's sexual proclivities, and she considered the events of that single evening an aberration. She'd never told Dim or anyone else about that. Dim was not liberal-minded about sexual deviation. He'd been more entertained by Tracy's account of the senator's problems with a prominent Godfather in the Mafia who was her uncle by marriage. Dim thought that was hilarious. He had no idea why the senator had ended her life, and while he considered it sad and unfortunate, he saw no reason for Tracy to feel responsible for her death.

"I did hear," he mentioned, "that there was a—a diagnosis recently. Someone said the outlook was not good. Poor woman."

Tracy seized on this. "You mean she really was ill? Was it cancer?"

"I have no idea," Dim said truthfully. "I merely heard a rumor that she might not run for office again. That would seem to fit, would it not?"

Tracy nodded sadly. "I suppose so. How terrible for her. I feel bad that I hadn't talked to her in a long time."

She was relieved. She didn't want to feel guilty about what had happened to Eleanor. Tracy had developed a certain indifference to political misfortune, because she thought much of it was self-inflicted, but she was far from callous, and Dim knew that. He had invented the rumor about the senator's illness as a means of easing Tracy's mind. He didn't want her sunny temperament shadowed by rumors over what she might not have done.

Dim was enjoying the brouhaha over the contents of *Listen!* magazine. He knew most of the cast of suspects involved and had little sympathy for any of them. He knew, too, that Tracy could have revealed more, because much of what she had confided in him had been left out. Tracy would not have been as forthcoming if she had not been hurt and angered by the attempts on her life by her erstwhile friends. He noted that she did well in television interviews, giving the impression of a woman whose beauty concealed a shrewd intellect and excellent memory, who had simply cashed in on what she knew. She insisted that most of her revelations about Washington had been secret only because nobody took the trouble to look for them. According to Tracy's version, such topics had been discussed at dinner parties she attended.

"People talked about these things. Nobody said they were secrets," she asserted.

She refused, however, to elaborate on the hints she had dropped about the sexual recreations of the politically powerful.

"People are entitled to personal privacy," she said, and insisted that this viewpoint was reconcilable with her allusions to eccentricity in the bedroom. All she was saying, she explained, was that politicians and diplomats were human. Such remarks were pounced on by President Potter and the Russian ambassador as evidence she could not prove what they called her vicious and unfounded slanders. Tracy read their rejoinders with amusement, accompanied by a reflection that had they not gone to such extreme measures to silence her, she wouldn't have put it into print at all.

Potter was beginning to think he might scrape through to reelection, having weathered, by a combination of humiliating candor and stone-faced toughness, the worst press conference he'd ever endured. There had also been a backlash to Tracy's book, with interviews with some of the men who'd been her great and good friends, as well as some of the women who hadn't been her friends at all. The trashing of Tracy was contributed to by her ex-husband,

Tommy, who, unreasonably, held her responsible for the disintegration of his relationship with Raymond. Tommy displayed almost total recall of Tracy's extramarital activities, which damaged her credibility.

The press, of course, had a wonderful time with the story they called Tracygate. It had everything from political scandal to sexual high jinks, so that investigative journalists could scrabble happily through the mud while the columnists poked fun and pontificated.

In the midst of it, Tracy and Dim decided to get married. It was Dim's idea, because he was becoming bored with Tracy's literary life. He had business abroad and he wanted her with him. But first he wanted an idyllic honeymoon on his island. Tracy resisted mildly because of book publication parties.

"Jerry wants me around for that," she said.

Dim frowned. "I don't care what Jerry wants," he said. "You have written the book as Mortimer wanted. It obviously is a success and it will be a success whether you are here or not. If it is absolutely necessary, we could come back for a visit. But I have waited, my darling. I let you keep your promise to Clayton Clapper, and now I want you to myself."

Tracy looked at him adoringly and curled into the wide circle of his arms. "Dim, darling," she said, "you've been so patient and I'm being selfish. We'll do anything in the world you want."

Dim kissed her. "Good," he said. "Then we shall be married next Tuesday. Then we go to my island."

"Next Tuesday?" said Tracy. "But my dress—"

"That gives you four days to get a dress," he said. "And I personally am much more interested in what is under the dress."

The announcement of their forthcoming marriage received considerable attention in the press and was read with particular attention in certain quarters in Chicago.

Dim said he would permit only photographers and a few questions after the ceremony in a small, exclusive Washington hotel.

"They can have ten minutes," he said. "Then you are gone forever."

Tracy didn't argue. She'd discovered Dim went along with whatever she wanted as long as she didn't contradict what he said he wanted at the time. She was caught up in a flurry of farewell parties given by some new friends, who were effusive but careful about what they said in front of her. She didn't care, because now she had Dim, who had even agreed that their best man would be Clayton Clapper. Clayton had returned to work with a vastly enhanced reputation and a considerably increased salary. Dim had come to admire Clayton's writing, but he could never warm to a man who couldn't handle a firearm. Rosemarie, of course, was to be maid of honor and, to console her for not accompanying the newlyweds to Dim's island, was being given a world cruise.

The ceremony was brief. Tracy was a vision in drifting creamy chiffon and pale pink roses, Rosemarie was radiant in delphinium blue, and Dim and Clayton were uncomfortable in morning suits. Dim glowered through a press conference that wound up lasting considerably less than ten minutes. Then he whisked Tracy through a side door, past a shower of rose petals tossed by Rosemarie and Clayton, and into a waiting limousine.

The limousine disappeared around a corner, and the wedding party returned to a lavish reception. The press, invited as a sop for not being allowed to ask questions, had less than fifteen minutes to relax. Press beepers began to sound, and reporters received emergency calls from their respective offices.

The explosion that blew up the limousine carrying Tracy and Dim smashed the windows in two nearby houses, and almost demolished a garage. By the time the fire department, police, and ambulances arrived, there wasn't much to be done. The flames of the explosion had reduced the car to twisted metal, and of its passengers and driver there was not a trace. As one television reporter put it, standing in front of the blackened wreckage, "This was the atomic weapon of car bombs. Experts are saying it was only by luck that more damage was not done to the surrounding area and that no one else was killed."

In Chicago, Francis Sikorski telephoned his congratulations to his old friend in the murder business. "Couldn't have done it better myself," he said, offering his highest praise.

"Any time," said the assassin, who had just banked a check well into six figures.

"Who did it?" President Potter inquired of the director of the CIA.

"Not us," said the director emphatically. "But they were certainly professionals."

"Too bad they didn't get hired sooner," the First Lady said coldly.

Tracygate was not over, but the death of the author and her most powerful supporter diminished the political strength of her charges. It was even easier to mock and disparage the claims of a dead Tracy.

However, from a publicity standpoint the tragedy titillated public interest in the book and resulted in a contract for a television movie, for which Clayton Clapper was hired as the screenwriter. Clayton, although genuinely grief-stricken over Tracy's death, was grateful to her for, in effect, extending a helpful financial hand from beyond the grave. With any luck, his accountant estimated, Clayton would never have to rely on a newspaper salary again.

"It was a privilege to know her," Clayton said brokenly at a memorial service for Tracy and Dim.

"A great lady," said Robert Mortimer, who was contemplating an instant biography of Tracy to cash in on her publicity and the investigation of the bombing, which apparently had gone nowhere.

In the nation's capital, there was an almost tangible easing of tension as Tracy faded into political lore and Sam Potter squeaked through to reelection. Yet Tracy was not entirely forgotten. There were moments at dinner parties when a politically prominent guest would realize he had been holding forth on a sensitive topic while simultaneously gazing into the wide and attentive eyes of a beautiful young woman who was giving him her full attention. And he would pause—and reflect.

Epilogue

The sun glinted on the gleaming white house, which seemed to flow into the pale sand ribboned by clear blue water. Servants moved silently across inlaid floors, and the only sound was a faint, rhythmical clicking. The sound came from a computer set up on a pink-tiled terrace beside a lily pond. At the computer sat a slender woman, her face almost concealed under the wide brim of a pink straw hat. She looked up and smiled as a hand fell on her tanned bare shoulder.

"Darling," she said.

The man leaned down and kissed her, then laughed as he read the words scrolled across the dark green screen.

"You made a decision," he said, stroking her arm.

The woman nodded. "I still can't believe it," she said reflectively.

"Believe what?"

"Switching cars. It never occurred to me."

The man laughed again and changed the subject. "What are you going to call it?" he asked.

The woman gave a little giggle as she fed the computer instructions to save what she had written. "*The Sequel,*" Tracy said softly. "That's what I'm going to call it. Just *The Sequel*."